Parent Involvement in Early Childhood Education

Revised Edition

Alice S. Honig
Syracuse University Children's Center

National Association for the Education of Young Children
Washington, D.C.

This work is an expanded version of workshops presented at the Merrill-Palmer Conference on Research and Teaching of Infant Development, Detroit, Michigan, February 1973, and the annual conference, "Priorities for Children," of the Southern Association on Children Under Six (SACUS), Louisville, Kentucky, April 1974. Profound thanks are expressed to Dr. Bettye M. Caldwell and to Dr. J. Ronald Lally for a critical reading of this manuscript. Their experience and wisdom have been of inestimable value.

Photos © 1979:
  Rick Reinhard *viii*
  Mary K. Gallagher *14*
  Rich Rosenkoetter *44*
  Florence Sharp *70*

Cover Design: Linda Kessler, Washington, D.C.

Second Printing, May 1976. Revised Edition, 1979.

Library of Congress Card Catalog Number: 75-3788
ISBN No. 0-912674-70-9

Printed in the United States of America.

For my children

Lawrence, Madeleine, and Jonathan,

who have made parent involvement in their education

such a deep joy.

Parent Involvement

Table of Contents

Introduction

Ira Gordon (1969a) has conceptualized parents' possible involvement in early education at several different levels.

1. Parents as an audience (passive role—conferences, newsletters, etc.).
2. Parents as a reference (active role—insights and perspectives on their child).
3. Parents as the teacher of the child.
4. Parents as volunteers in the classroom.
5. Parents as trained/paid aides.
6. Parents as participants in the decision-making process.

Salient comments have been made with regard to the social and community aspects of parent involvement at the decision-making level.

Parental involvement has been an antidote to professional arrogance by dramatically spotlighting the parents' role in the developmental process.

It has played a crucial role in linking the child's home/community world with his formal learning environment.

It has challenged us to think critically about parents' rights to participate in decisions affecting their children.

Parental involvement, at its best, means that parents
have become evaluators of the quality of programming
for their children. (Day Care Council of Westchester
1974, Summary of Knitzer's remarks, p. 5)

This survey, however, will not focus on parents who already are active participators in child learning or those who are active in decision-making processes within educational settings for their children. Such roles as change agents imply the prior attainment by parents of skills, interest in and involvement with child education. Nor will we deal with community, professional, political, and institutional prejudices or insensitivities, which often thwart parent involvement at an advisory and decision-making level.

Rather, our concern will be with those program models and methods which are attempting to promote parental involvement with early child development and education. We will also examine some of the difficulties, successes, and insights encountered in the parent involvement process.

ALICE S. HONIG

1

Basic Child-Education Knowledge: A Parent's Right

There are basic childrearing tools which are at least as important to parents as the usual carpentry or cooking tools available in most households. Citizens have a right to such tools for optimizing parenting just as they have a right to literacy and job skills for work and participation in our society.

Knowledge About Child Development

No matter at which level they are involved in their children's learning careers, parents need knowledge about how children develop. Normative patterns and stages in physical, social, language, and sexual development as well as nutritional and health needs at these stages should be part of the knowledge base for parenthood. Knowing that an infant triples his or her birth weight in the first year of life and that the growth rate then slows considerably can be valuable information, for example, to a parent bewildered by a poor appetite in a two-year-old who ate so ravenously when he was much younger. Knowing when a baby can be expected to begin to have some voluntary control over the sphincter muscles for elimination, or over voluntary release of an object grasped in the hand may encourage more enlightened and less punitive assessments of noncompliance by young children.

Knowledge of emotional needs and typical early social-emotional behaviors may similarly forestall inappropriate parental responses to common emotional responses of young children. Knowing the stages of cognitive development should help parents form more realistic expectations of the sequences of development and the prior understandings required for more mature cognitive competencies.

Observation Skills and More Effective Parenting

Another basic need of all parents, regardless of their income or education, is to learn how to observe a young child. Informal child-watching can help one figure out where a child is developmentally—socially, intellectually, perceptually, emotionally, motorically—in relation to what one would like a young child to learn or accomplish. In essence, parents need information and observation skills to help them meet the problem of the "match" between child ability or readiness and some ways and means to help the child toward a given developmental goal. This "match" is important no matter what kind of developmental goal is desired or how trivial or important that goal may seem for either the parent or the child. For example, for a not too steady-handed baby, observant parents will supply a spoon *shaped comfortably* for baby's hand so that some unspilled cereal does reach baby's mouth. Very often parents choose toys in which they invest too much money and the child invests too little interest. Sharpened observation skills will make possible more toy choices appropriate to different stages of developmental interest and ability.

A corollary of becoming attuned to the "problem of the match" is becoming able to adjust creatively to a child's problems and goals in early learning in order either to ease a learning situation or to make it more challenging for a particular child. Such "tuning in" can help a parent handle child frustrations more skillfully in daily situations such as shoelace tying.

Alternative Strategies for Problem Prevention and for Discipline

Young couples are often showered with cookbooks which inform them of dozens of easy ways to prepare meals. More often parents more urgently need "recipes" for managing child behaviors. Knowledge of alternative methods of discipline and of problem avoidance is a basic childrearing tool. Wittes and Radin (1969) provide us with a delightful example of one such alternative strategy.

Johnny is racing around pretending he is a dog. The phone rings and you ask him to stop but he will not. What is your choice of strategies in this situation?

a. You can get mad at him and send him to his room in anger. As a rebellious four-year-old, he doesn't want to get "pushed around," and raises a terrible fuss, etc.

b. You can use dramatic play as a strategy. Excuse yourself from the phone for a minute and say, "You're barking so much, doggy, and making so much noise. Here is your bone. (Give him a block or a small book as a make-believe object.) Eat your bone quietly now and have a little snooze while I'm on the phone. After I get off the phone I'm going to teach you some new tricks for being a good doggy."

You see, you are moving right into the role-play here and creating a tolerable and fun-filled situation for your child. You are persuading him to be quiet through a playful approach which doesn't threaten him as it does when you order him to be quiet as his mother. He doesn't have to rebel against you because you and he are in a game together. You have changed his resistance into compliance. You have "saved face" for both of you. He has not refused to obey you. You have not humiliated him by your demands. (pp. 21-22)

Having a variety of positive rewards in one's repertoire can help a child to enjoy more fully explorations and struggles to achieve new mastery, new understanding. Joy in voice tone, a smile, ruffling the hair, a kiss or hug, a "good-for-you" clap of the hands—these are but a few of the ways parents can express their responsiveness to and appreciation of child-sized trials and triumphs.

How to Use a Home for Learning Experiences

Another basic tool consists of knowing how to take advantage of settings, routines, and activities in the home to create learning and problem-solving opportunities for children as well as sociable experiences. Cooking times are wonderful times to have children learn words like *stir, turn, wash, mix, taste.* Laundry sorting provides untold problems to solve—matching socks, classifying clothing pieces into piles, folding assorted linens into different shapes and sizes. Parents of preschoolers need to know ways of turning household discards into learning materials for children's explorations. Such tips on the use of "beautiful junk" (Warner and Quill 1969) could be published by local newspapers in the same way they offer daily household tips for home repairs and for preparing inexpensive nutritious meals.

Parents Need Language Tools

How does one simplify explanations to make sense of the world for a preschool child, or return happy talk in response to a baby's unintelligible babbling and to sometimes misshapen early words? How does one relate language to picture books to whet an appetite for reading experiences at an early age? How does one ensure that language experiences are positive, instead of negative as when words are used mainly to give orders or express irritation? What kinds of language games will help a child enjoy the pleasures of naming? The parent who has learned to give names to the things a child notices, to the actions a child carries out, and to the feeling a child expresses has a powerful tool for helping the child advance in language skills.

Parents Are Important People

Most of all, parents need to feel how much they make a difference in their children's lives. Their paying attention, their pleasure expressed, their listening, their interest—all nourish the growing self of the child as food nourishes his or her body and as toys and sights, sounds, and smells nourish the senses. Not only their importance to their children should be clarified and given specific meaning, but also the opportunity such interactions give them personally for finding pleasure and interest in their relationships with their own and with others' children.

2

Emphasis on Parent Involvement

Parent involvement has in the last few years become the magic phrase to be intoned at the birth of new early child care projects in order to ensure long life and success to the newborn projects. This conviction that parent involvement is essential to program success, for example, led to the directives for inclusion of parents in all phases of project functioning for Head Start. The cornerstone of planning for new national programs such as Parent-Child Centers (Costello and Binstock 1970) and Home Start has been the concept of involving parents in their children's early learning. Federal Interagency Day Care guidelines (1968) for parental involvement now mandate quite specifically that:

* Parents must have the opportunity to become involved themselves in the making of decisions concerning the nature and operation of the day care facility.

* Parents must be provided with opportunities at times convenient to them to work with the program and whenever possible to observe their children in the day care facility.

* Whenever an agency provides day care for 40 or more children, there must be a Policy Advisory Committee. Committee membership should include not less than 50 percent parents or parent representatives, selected by the parents themselves.

In the guidelines for Parent-Child Centers (Office of Child Development 1968), potential participants are *required* to have a voice in the decision-making process. Parents who function on the Policy Advisory Committees are expected to:

(1) Assist in the development of and give approval to the application before it is submitted.

(2) Participate in the selection of the Staff Director. Decisions on selection of a Staff Director should reflect a consensus between the Policy Advisory Committee and the administering agency. The formal appointment action should follow whatever procedures are appropriate in the particular community.

(3) Have a voice in establishing criteria for the selection of staff personnel.

(4) Initiate suggestions and ideas for program improvements.

(5) Serve as a channel for hearing complaints on the program.

(6) Assist in organizing activities for parents.

(7) Assume some degree of responsibility for communicating with parents and encouraging their participation in the program.

(8) Serve as a link to public and private organizations.

(9) Represent organizations, clubs and agencies in the neighborhood and parents involved in the program.

(10) Aid in recruiting volunteers and assist in mobilizing community resources.

(11) Participate in the development of policies and procedures for the planning and operation of all phases of the PCC program.

Meetings must be frequent, with prepared agenda. One or two meetings during the course of the program is not sufficient. (pp. 49-50)

Yet directives to ensure parental involvement with program games and goals for children do not magically or quickly translate into effective communication and action systems to implement these directives. For example, Lazar and Chapman (1972), in their survey of programs to develop parenting skills, noted at the 1972 date of the report that although 32 of the 35 Parent-Child Centers (PCCs) had established Parent Policy Advisory Committees, only in 11 PCCs were parents taking an active part in regular meetings and in making major decisions. It should be noted that enforcement mechanisms, which could ensure rigorous attempts by early child care administrators to implement these guidelines, are weak.

The crucially important interrelationship of parental involvement as well as teacher involvement with children's learning careers was sometimes insufficiently taken into account a decade ago by pioneer planners of intervention programs for very young children from lower-socioeconomic milieux. These innovative programs, geared toward deficit prevention, often focused rather on other urgent problems such as the development of instructional goals, settings, and tasks appropriate for infants, toddlers, and preschoolers and on the development of trained personnel to work with young children toward such goals.

Yet, conceptualization of the characteristics of parent-child interactions (Schaefer 1972) suggests that, beside the primary responsibility borne for the child, parents have a relation with the child which exceeds that with other adults in priority, duration, continuity, amount, extensity, intensity, pervasiveness, and consistency. Therefore, "the continuation of these different characteristics of parent-child interaction suggests that their cumulative impact upon the child's development would be substantial" (p. 228).

Additionally, as Lally (1969a) has pointed out from teacher reports, family factors such as sickness, death, power struggles, or frequent changes in number of members in the household may have a great effect on program performance of a young child and should certainly be of concern to those responsible for a young child's learning in an educational setting.

Of course parent involvement with a child's learning career has been long perceived by school teachers of older children as an integral factor in a child's school success. Indeed, teachers have often lamented that the interested parents who show up for PTA meetings or for open school nights are just those involved parents the teachers don't feel they need to see. The interactions of teachers themselves with parents have been found to affect children's learning. Beller's (1969) research on teacher attitudes has shown that where teachers "exhibited greater respect than other teachers for the child's family" (p. 39) this was associated with a child's readiness to gain from educational experiences in the classroom.

Impetus for Present Emphasis on Parent Involvement

Three historical trends are largely responsible for the recent urgent reactivation of interest and realization of the importance of involving parents in early child care programs. Accumulative research data have given impetus to a growing awareness of the basic and critical nature of parent involvement for producing healthy, happy, and active child-learners, regardless of whether those learners are yet in some sort of more formal child care or schooling system, or in the primary care of parents and parent surrogates.

Dissipation of Intervention Effects Where Parents Weren't Involved

The first historical stream feeding the present rushing tide to involve parents in their children's learning stems from the undisputed failure of almost all intervention programs without such involvement to sustain the often considerable cognitive gains demonstrated during the child's participation in such a program.

Failure to *maintain* cognitive gains where parent involvement was minimal or nonsystematic has been found regardless of the theoretical orientation or curricular format of the program. Thus Schaefer's tutorial at-home model with low-income Washington, D.C., infants, Caldwell's omnibus day care model at Syracuse, and Bereiter-Engelmann's model of pattern-drill lessons for low-income preschoolers in specific cognitive skill areas have all demonstrated quite encouraging cognitive gains for participating children in comparison with controls, and then declines over time in these accrued advantages. The conviction that parent involvement remains an indispensable ingredient for sustaining program accomplishments after a young child's participation in an early education program has led experts to affirm that "to work with children alone is to invite failure and frustration" (Biber 1970, p. 1).

Cultural and Familial Differences

A second source of data consists of observed cultural and familial differences in parent-child interactions. Research into parent-child exchanges tends to point up differences in the abilities of parents to teach their own children effectively (Baumrind 1967; Bayley and Schaefer 1960; Bee, Van Egeren, Pytkowitz, Nyman, and Leckie 1969; Bing 1963; Hess, Shipman, Brophy, and Bear 1968; Hindley 1962; Hubner 1970; Marans and Lourie 1967; Radin and Kamii 1965; Shere and Kastenbaum 1966; Slaughter 1968; Streissguth and Bee 1972; Wortis et al. 1963). Brophy (1970) has demonstrated that maternal teaching styles vary widely, from limited reactive teaching with use of controls and demands, to effective use of suggestions and instructions. Olmstead and Jester (1972) have further analyzed maternal-child teaching interactions to discover the dimensions along which such interactions differ. For example, more middle-socioeconomic class mothers in their study provided advanced organizing information about a block-sorting task. These mothers made such clarifying statements as "We are going to learn how to sort these blocks." The mothers not only provided more detailed introductions to the learning

8

task but provided more verbal variety and more explanations or reasons for their corrections of a child's responses. Low-income mothers in this study predominantly used such controls as threats or physical restraints when children were corrected.

Milner (1951) interviewed mothers and children and found that children who achieved higher language scores on the California Test of Mental Maturity were read to more often, had more mealtime conversation with parents, received less harsh physical punishment, and were predominantly from middle-socioeconomic class families. Such obtained differences have led Strodbeck (1965) to refer to a "hidden curriculum" in the middle-socioeconomic class home.

There is, of course, a large range of variability of behaviors within any such gross designation as "socioeconomic class." In Gordon's home visitation project, the amount of conversation in the home, particularly that directed toward the child, related significantly to child performance on developmental tests (Jester and Bailey 1969; Resnick 1973), yet all parents and children involved were from low-income families.

Lesser, Fifer, and Clark (1965) have reported that ethnic background and socioeconomic class have different effects. Similarities in the *patterns* of verbal, spatial, numerical, and reasoning scores for two socioeconomic class levels of a given ethnic group were found. The groups also showed pronounced score differences between socioeconomic classes, with middle-socioeconomic class first grade children significantly superior to lower-socioeconomic class children in all four ethnic groups sampled.

Importance of family process variables. In measuring aspects of the environment which correlate with the growth of intelligence and academic achievement, Wolf (1964) and Davé (1963) have made a distinction between *status* and *process* variables. *Status* variables are demographic such as income and education level. *Process* variables relate to intellectual expectations of parents for a child and amount of intellectual facilitation provided.

Wolf has related family process variables to child intelligence and Davé has related the process variables to achievement. They found multiple correlations of .76 and .80 respectively with these child measures when they used predictors such as quality of maternal language, amount of reading and conversation, opportunity for the child to learn new words, and cultural level of home discussions. Linnan and Arassian (1974) have more recently analyzed family home interview and observation data in two different ethnic groups. Ratings based on maternal language style items had the highest multiple correlation (R=.61) with child's verbal ability. Mothers' language was rated by complexity of words, use of abstract rather than concrete speech, conversational context, and amount and regularity of reading to the child.

Schaefer's (1972) review of a variety of longitudinal as well as cross-sectional studies indicates that family process was found to be more highly related to intelligence and achievement than was socioeconomic status. In studies where socioeconomic level of the family was controlled, "children's test scores were much more related to degree of parent interest than to variations in the quality of the schools" (p. 234).

There is increasing awareness of the importance of parents in influencing a child's academic motivation. Zigler (1970) has analyzed how important familial-cultural experiences are to a child's educational achievement motivation and emotional systems.

> First, a well-documented phenomenon ... is that children who do not receive enough affection and attention from the important adults in their life suffer in later years from an atypically high need for such attention and affection. When faced with cognitive tasks, such children do not appear highly motivated to solve the intellectual problems confronting them but rather employ their interactions with adults to satisfy hunger for attention, affection, and yes, as unscientific as it may be, their need for love. We have conducted longitudinal studies of children who were socially deprived in the first few years of life and we still find the effects of the early deprivation experiences some ten years later . . . .
>
> Note the problem that such children present to their teachers. Instead of attending to a curriculum task and solving it, the child may whine and ask the teacher to solve the task for him. The teacher tuned in only to the cognitive aspects of the situation concludes the child is unintelligent. On the other hand, the teacher who realizes how depriving experiences spell themselves out in the motivational structure of the child may more correctly conclude that what is interfering with the child's performance is his need for a positive interaction with an adult. If we appreciate the child's emotional needs and attempt to satisfy them, we would not be surprised to see the child then go on to a better school performance. (p. 410)

Studies which have revealed that some parental teaching styles, language interactions, and cognitive expectations are not conducive toward providing what Caldwell (1967) has dubbed the "opti-

10

mal learning environment'' for a young child have stimulated thinking about ways to enrich parent-child learning interactions and have galvanized early childhood project leaders to rethink their more narrowly conceived "intervention" efforts in order to include parent involvement as *crucial* to successful educational outcomes for young children.

Positive Parenting and Child Competence

The third factor which has strengthened the present growing commitment to parent involvement in children's education is accumulating positive evidence of the effectiveness of parent involvement in young children's education in influencing academic motivation (Willmon 1969).

Research on the effects of positive parenting practices in maternal home-rearing situations has added to our information base (Yarrow, Rubenstein, and Pederson 1971). Beckwith's (1972) observations of adoptive mothers with infants revealed that high frequency of maternal physical and verbal contacts and low restrictiveness for an infant's explorations were associated with significantly higher Cattell IQ scores.

Extensive observations by Watts, Barnett, and Halfar (1973) of the interactions of families of varying social backgrounds with their babies in the natural course of development over several years eloquently support the above findings. "As early as the age of 24 to 27 months the experiences of certain of these children who develop very well intellectually; ('A' children) and others who do not ('C' children) differ strikingly. Mothers, fathers, babysitters and other people who are in contact with these A children spend more time interacting with them in the context of intellectually stimulating activities, more time directly participating in these activities, and more selectively encouraging these activities than interactors with C children" (pp. 186-187). These data were found for all of the families involved, regardless of socioeconomic class status.

Swan and Stavros (1973) inquired about parental practices in 40 Black, low-income families whose five- and six-year-old children exhibited effective learning styles in school.

> These children have the quality of being able to listen and use information from adults and other children alike, although they work independently without prodding. They are not afraid to try new games and activities,

11

are willing to take reasonable risks, and usually demonstrate an attitude of self-confidence. Usually they are in control of situations and can channel energy toward the activities of the program from which they gain considerable mastery and pleasure. They often create their own opportunities for satisfaction. Their main concern is enjoyment in doing for the sake of doing rather than to please someone or to get external rewards. They ask meaningful and appropriate questions, describe their experiences colorfully, and have a noticeable sense of humor. They are exuberant when they arrive at their own solutions to problems and can look at their own performance objectively and learn from efforts. These children are usually successful in resolving conflicts that arise with other children. Although they (the children) require little discipline, teachers are usually well aware of who they are. (p. 27)

The parents' philosophy included encouraging independence of the children and understanding and respecting the child's feelings and point of view. They expressed feelings of competence in raising their children. The parents fostered independence in the children by giving them responsibilities around the home. They described their children "in a very positive and competent light. . . . Most of the parents talked with their children about a wide range of topics in a variety of contexts, and shared many verbal episodes that were mutually pleasant" (pp. 34-35). All but three of the parents read to and discussed stories with their children.

Parents in a rural Head Start program participated in a weekly parent education group with specific emphasis on language training for their children. The mothers increased their verbal skills as well as the quality of their interactions with their children. The children developed a more positive perception of their mother's view of them and performed higher on verbal intelligence subtests of the Wechsler Preschool and Primary Scale of Intelligence (Kuipers, Boger, and Beery 1970).

Parent involvement and continuing educational gains. There is increasing and consistent evidence that parental participation is the key to *sustaining* gains achieved in early childhood programs.

A survey of Head Start parents has found a positive relationship between extensive parent participation and children's scores which reflect better task orientation, academic achievement, verbal intelligence, and self-concept. The amount of parent participation seemed of far more importance than the kind of model or structure

12

within which participation occurred. Parents who participated a great deal saw themselves as more successful and skillful. Additionally, after the termination of the Head Start experience, their activities in other community events rose to higher levels than those existent prior to Head Start experiences (MIDCO 1972).

Summary of Research Evidence on Parent Participation— and Prescriptions

After an in-depth survey of the effects of a variety of intervention programs—some with and some without parent participation—Bronfenbrenner (1974) strongly concluded:

> The evidence indicates that the family is the most effective and economical system for fostering and sustaining the development of the child. The evidence indicates further than the involvement of the child's family as an active participant is critical to the success of any intervention program. Without such family involvement, any effects of intervention, at least in the cognitive sphere, are likely to be ephemeral, to appear to erode rapidly once the program ends. In contrast, the involvement of the parents as partners in the enterprise provides an on-going system which can reinforce the effects of the program while it is in operation, and help to sustain them after the program ends. (p. 55)

Schaefer (1973) too has surveyed the effects of intervention programs and concluded that a more comprehensive definition of education is necessary. Such a redefinition then leads to a major new objective for professional educators in order

> to influence the child's education in the home, community, and through the mass media from birth onward —before school entrance, evenings, weekends, holidays, vacations, and after the school years. This objective would require that educators involve themselves in training parents and future parents in family care and education skills. . . . The ability of the family to care for and educate the child is weakened by stresses and strengthened by support from neighbors, friends, relatives, social groups, and relevant professionals. . . . If the education profession could develop new roles they might provide training and experience in child care and education to future parents throughout the period of

13

school attendance and also provide methods, materials, training, and consultation to parents of school-age children. Training and support for family care and education of the child before school entrance might be provided by health personnel, by educators, or by a new discipline. . . .

Ideally, professional education will provide support for family education of the child. . . . Schools are necessary but not sufficient for the education of the child. (pp. 9-10)

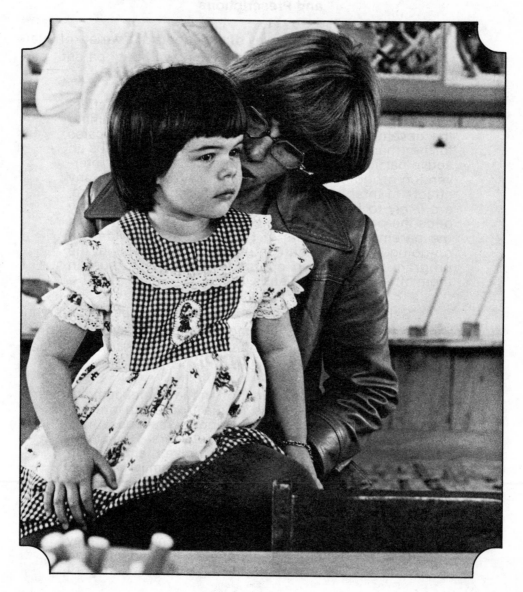

3

Ways in Which Parents Are Being Involved in Early Childhood Programs

Partly in response to research findings about parent needs, and certainly in response to a theoretical belief in the indispensability of positive parental involvement in child development and education, a variety of program models and services have been developed to foster such parental involvement.

A survey of ways in which parents are participating in child care programs provides confirmation of the variety of efforts undertaken, problems encountered, and successes achieved. Institutions and projects have actively sought to increase parent involvement in children's development and learning by a wealth of innovative program efforts.

Home Visitation Only

This model arose partly because of the economies to be gained by home visitation programs without additional day or nursery care, and because there are theoretical objections by some professionals to the removal of a very young child from the home for any kind of group care. Several projects have used this model systematically.

Bringing games and "know-how" to parents. The "Infant Stimulation through Family Life Education" program in Albany, New York (Ligon, Barber, and Williams 1971), and Ira Gordon's (1971) home visitation program in Florida have involved paraprofessionals. Tom Ryan's (1972) home visitation program in Canada has enlisted volunteers. Through demonstration and practice, the visitors teach mothers at home. The home visitors teach mothers how to provide facilitating sensorimotor experiences and language games for their infants. Particularly emphasized are ways in which parents can use daily interactions and caregiving situations with infants to create learning occasions and opportunities. Exercises and games appropriate to the level of development of the baby are taught each week; sample fact sheets describing the purpose of each new game and ways to carry out the game are left with the mothers. The home visitor focuses on the parent as the important person to work with rather than the baby.

The Ypsilanti-Carnegie Infant Education Project (Lambie 1973; Lambie, Bond, and Weikart 1974) has as its main developmental objective the construction of a Piagetian-based curriculum for increasing a mother's awareness of and her ability to enhance her infant's cognitive growth.

At the George Peabody College Demonstration and Research Center for Early Education (DARCEE), Susan Gray (1971) and Bettye Jean Forrester (1972) have been active in developing home visitation techniques and tasks for mothers of preschoolers. DARCEE's goal has been to provide mothers with the coping skills and assurance they need to handle the entire job of being their preschool children's teacher. Parents are seen as educational change agents for their own infants and children. The DARCEE study has also highlighted the economic and programmatic advantages of using paraprofessionals as home visitors (Barbrack and Horton 1970a, 1970b).

Levenstein's (1970) Verbal Interaction Project is based on the conviction that parents can be given the "know-how" and the encouragement to stimulate their children's intellectual development through verbal interactions. Levenstein (1971a, 1971b, 1972) stresses the importance of training and supervision in the success of the home visitors called Toy Demonstrators. This program has registered gains in children's developmental scores on successive years when the home visitors were either middle-socioeconomic class volunteers or paraprofessionals who had earlier been recipients themselves of this home visitation program.

> *Toy demonstrators.* The toy demonstrators are selected on liberal criteria and receive special training before beginning to work. . . . The toy demonstrator's role requires development of a warm relationship with the mother and child, demonstration of verbal stimulation techniques, and the development of maximum mother participation. The toy demonstrator visits each pair

twice a week for a half-hour home session. On the first visit each week she brings either a toy or a book which she uses as a Verbal Interaction Stimulus Material. She introduces the VISM to the child, encouraging him to talk by asking him questions, listening to his answers, and replying. At the same time she draws the mother into the session by modeling verbal stimulation techniques, which the mother then imitates. She also encourages the mother to read and play with the child between home sessions.

Verbal Interaction Stimulus Materials (VISM). The 11 toys and 12 books used each year to stimulate verbal interaction within the mother-child relationship are presented to the child as gifts, one each week in alternating order. During their initial session, the mother and the toy demonstrator cooperate in putting together a special toy chest designed to store the VISM. (p. 7)

Home visitation for the handicapped. Home visitation has the advantage of being able to be tailored to the ecology and circumstances unique to each child. This may be particularly useful when a target child is handicapped or lives in an isolated area. Home teachers in the Wisconsin Portage Project (Shearer and Shearer 1972) provide parents with activities for multi-handicapped preschoolers.

Parents are taught how to keep daily frequency records of behaviors being learned. They are taught what to teach, what to reinforce, and how to shape behaviors by the technique of initially providing and then "fading out" reinforcements. The child is assigned an individualized goal which can be achieved in one week regardless of severity of handicap. One such goal may be to succeed in hopping on one foot without support five times per trial with three trials daily. The home teacher leaves materials to be used, written instructions and charts to record progress. Parents are the prime informants and the key to project success. The home teacher draws on resources the parent has at hand for ideas for increasing a child's experiences, discoveries, and skills. The home teacher meets the mother on territory she is familiar with and that she is in charge of—her own home.

Home visitation with fathers. The home visitation model has predominantly been carried out by female workers with mothers. However, Bowles and Scheinfeld (1969), in an experimental effort with a small number of low-income families in an urban housing project, found that fathers could be more actively involved in their children's educational experience when male workers tailored the home visitation program specially for the fathers. Tuck (1969) has suggested a model for working with Black fathers.

Home visitation and the power position of the teaching person. Far different power relationships with parents may exist for the "expert" in a home-teaching program than may be the case where an institution is the setting for the interaction. Weikart (1969) has specified some of the subtle and not-so-subtle differences in the dynamics of home visitation work versus teaching in school settings.

Teachers working in the homes of disadvantaged families must accept a role different from that assumed when working in traditional classroom or clinical settings. Professionally, teachers are trained to work with groups that are basically captive audiences making the sacrifice and effort to be present and assuming low "power" positions, i.e., sitting at desks, answering roll calls, performing to teacher expectations, etc. In addition, classroom teachers seldom have their performance judged in any immediate way other than being "liked or disliked" by their students. Only occasionally is long-term achievement by students introduced as a possible consideration of teaching effectiveness. Home teaching, on the other hand, demands a very different performance on the part of the teacher. Acceptance of a position of low power, immediate critical evaluation of teaching, and adjustment to economic and social differences are all required of the teachers.

The teacher is a guest in the home of a mother. As a guest, the teacher must sit where told to sit and put up with many inconveniences, e.g., dirt, bugs, disease, poor heating, lack of work space, lack of access to teaching supplies, assorted visitors viewing the teaching, summary dismissal by the mother, cancellations of appointments by the mother, etc. In all of this the teacher basically assumes a position of low power.

In addition, the mother does an immediate evaluation of the teacher's performance during the working session. In the classroom the teacher is seldom judged in areas other than discipline and classroom management. In the home, trial and error teaching is not well received and negative reaction is immediate to teaching failure. The teacher must demonstrate that she can tap the child's ability, handle teaching situations correctly, and explain why something did or didn't work. If she fails in any of these categories, she seldom receives a second chance unless the mother is convinced of the teacher's expertise. (pp. 28-29)

Manuals and materials. Helpful guides to assist families and parent educators in boosting infant, toddler, and preschooler development have emerged from home visitation programs. Many of the activities and materials recommended have been field-tested in homes: Adkins 1971b; Bromwich 1976; Bromwich et al. 1978; Forrester, Brooks, Hardge, and Outlaw 1971; Forrester, Hardge, Outlaw, Brooks, and Boismier 1971; Giesy 1970; Gordon 1970a; Gordon, Guinagh, and Jester 1972; Gordon and Lally 1967; Lambie 1972; Levenstein 1973; Segner and Patterson 1970.

Parent Group Meetings

The parent involvement model which relies exclusively on parent group meetings has been used by many programs with widely differing goals. Programs which teach parents in groups have sometimes opted for cognitive emphasis—teaching mothers how to improve children's language skills, for example. Other parent groups have focused on increasing parental self-awareness (Adkins 1971a), knowledge of ways to motivate children, or expression of parental needs (Stern, Marshall, and Edwards 1971), home management skills, or making and learning to use inexpensive home learning materials (Karnes, Studley, Wright, and Hodgins 1968).

Karnes, Hodgins, Teska, and Kirk (1969) carried out parent group meetings with mothers of children not attending any preschool. Under these conditions paid participation by one group of mothers in twelve two-hour parent-education sessions had positive effects on their children's intellective growth in comparison to control children with nonparticipating mothers.

Toy lending and demonstrating. Nimnicht's (1972) Far West Parent/Child Toy Library Program has involved parents in eight two-hour sessions, usually meeting once a week. Child development topics are discussed and a new toy introduced at each meeting. The toy as a means to boost children's problem-solving skills is demonstrated, discussed, and illustrated in films. Parents at the group meeting role-play with each other ways to use toys so that their youngsters can later be helped to make discoveries on their own as they play with the toys.

Stevens (1973) has reported that an eleven-week program of small group parent meetings which included toy/book demonstration and lending produced significant IQ gains for children of project participants. He suggests that the parent consultants would have been even more effective had they provided feedback to a parent during his or her interaction with a child in the home.

Language facilitation through parent meetings. An interesting and more specifically-focused parent group program was set

19

up with Mexican-American mothers in an Arizona Follow-Through program (Garcia 1972). These mothers were trained by modeling techniques to help their first graders ask more questions, particularly during storybook time. Mothers role-played with each other, learned to use cueing techniques to initiate a child's question-asking, to use contingent praise, and to use hand counters to record the numbers of questions asked by their children. Later, mothers learned to reward causal questions particularly. Many mothers became aware of the potential importance of a child's talking and asking questions through this procedure. Mothers and older siblings seemed to gain much pleasure both from helping young children in the family improve their questioning skills and from the "click-off" monitoring system.

One parent group meeting plan to help parents encourage language development from infancy onward is called "Teach Your Child to Talk" (Pushaw 1969). The parent workshops are carefully programmed with slides, cassette-illustrated vocalization examples, and written materials for workshop leaders.

Audiovisual materials for parent education. A number of new audiovisual materials are now available for working with parents in groups. High/Scope (1978) has created several films appropriate for adult training. Concept Media (1973, 1975) and Parents' Magazine (1978) produce sound and color filmstrip sets designed to promote effective parenting. Concept Media also provides filmstrips on parent participation in child care programs. "Parenthood: A Series" consists of eight color and sound filmstrips and eight discussion guides and is available from Guidance Associates (1978).

A parent education television series (1978), "Footsteps," uses situations that dramatize "Parents' concerns about childrearing, the problems they encounter, and some possible solutions and coping strategies." Each program focuses on a particular theme designed to increase parents' knowledge and understanding of child development, enhance their skills in dealing with everyday experiences, and develop self-confidence and positive attitudes toward parenting.

See p. 100 for other available audiovisual materials.

Home Visits with Linkages to Nutrition, Health, Social, and Psychological Services and/or in Combination with Group Meetings

Home Start. Home Start (O'Keefe 1973b) has been launched as an adjunct to Head Start. This program is aimed at involving parents as the *major* means of helping the children, whereas Head

20

Start has used parent involvement as one means in addition to preschool programs. Sixteen localities each receive about $100,000 per year to serve 80 families. The objectives of the Home Start program are to strengthen in parents their capacity for facilitating the general development of their children and to involve parents directly in their children's educational development, as well as to demonstrate ways in which comprehensive Head Start type services to children can be delivered in a home-based program.

The qualifications emphasized in selecting a home visitor are "friendly attitudes, suitability of cultural and language background, and successful experience as a parent, rather than. . . academic credentials" (p. 3).

Typically, a Home Start visitor may help parents identify a goal which they already hold for the child, such as good health or readiness for school, and then introduce the parents to a neighborhood health clinic or to games and toys to help a preschooler with concepts he or she needs to know.

The range of jobs and activities which a home visitor does or arranges for is remarkable and impressive for variety and comprehensiveness. A home visitor may:

Introduce a toy (or book or creative experience) that will necessarily involve the parent in a developmental experience with the child.

Help the mother make homemade toys improvised from household items to foster development.

Help the mother with a household chore (such as washing dishes, making biscuits, or peeling potatoes) and, by involving the child, demonstrate how the activities which normally make up the fabric of each day can be used as constructive learning experiences for children.

Talk with the mother about each child and the things she is doing to further their development, praising her for gains made, and making occasional suggestions.

Introduce activities that involve the older children, or that encourage the older children to work with and help the younger ones.

Budget some time to give the mother an opportunity to talk about her own achievements, needs, or problems.

Take time from more serious purposes for a snack or sociable chat, perhaps while helping a busy mother dry dishes or fold diapers.

Read and evaluate the newspaper's food ads with mother.

Help mother make a shopping list.

Go food shopping with mother and child.

Assist family in taking steps to obtain donated or commodity foods.

Arrange for local home economists to demonstrate preparation of inexpensive but nourishing foods.

Cook supper with mother and child, showing mother (by example) how child can be involved—noting colors, textures, and shapes of food and kitchen equipment, counting eggs, spoons, etc., and talking.

Take mother with child for child's physical and dental examinations.

Set up appointments at free clinic for mother's physical examination.

Set up family first aid course for Home Start staff and parents.

Mark height of each family member on wall in home.

Arrange for exterminator to come.

Help parents assess home with regard to safety precautions—exposed poisons, electrical outlets, lead paint, etc.

Make sure that all follow-up health care is provided for identified health needs.

Call on local doctors to tell them about Home Start and ask their help.

Show mother how to check for worms.

Provide toothbrushing kits and instructions for all family members.

Read with mother the health columns in local newspapers.

Use local telephone book as a directory of resources, showing mother how resources are listed.

Take mother or parents to the resource facility, walking through entire process with parent(s).

Use "Parent Effectiveness Training" to prevent communications problems within families.

Help families team up with neighbors or relatives who own transportation.

Hold program-wide picnics or other social affairs for parents or entire families.

Take parents to local libraries and show shelves with books on child-rearing.

Arrange for Home Start staff and interested parents to take courses on child-rearing, such as "Parent Effectiveness Training."

Hold mothers' group meetings to use one another as resources in finding solutions to child-rearing problems.

Prepare simple guides to accompany children's television programs which are shown locally, to make television-watching less passive and more active.

Suggest ways to turn everyday events into learning experiences, such as going to the grocery store and playing a "color game" on the way or peeling vegetables and teaching the child size and color concepts at the same time.

Obtain films on child development or child-rearing to show to groups of parents.

Cut out pictures in magazines and help parents make games—classifying objects, counting, etc.

Obtain tools and materials such as plywood scraps and tri-wall, so parents (especially fathers and older brothers) can make wagons, insert puzzles, storage chests, bookshelves, and other items for their own families. (O'Keefe 1973b, pp. 4-11)

In its efforts to increase community participation, the Top of Alabama Regional Council of Government (TARCOG) Home Start program (1972) in five Alabama counties is even more ambitious. This program plans not only for visitor-parent interactions in the home, but interaction in parent group meetings and also interaction of parents, laymen, and professionals on a regional basis with interagency planning and sharing.

One advantage to Home Start is that it provides help to many families who have no access to preschool child development centers. Another advantage to Home Start is that direct and maximal benefits can accrue to *all* children in a family, not just to the target child enrolled, for example, in a preschool program.

Home Visit or Parent Group Meetings in Combination with Preschool Experiences for Children

A great many parent involvement efforts, such as those in Head Start, have served as adjuncts or outreach efforts to enhance the effectiveness of ongoing curricular and group experiences provided for young children (Adkins 1971a; Klaus and Gray 1968; Nimnicht 1970; Weikart 1971a). Research findings on the effects of such efforts have been uneven.

Adkins, for example, has found the combined effects of preschool plus parent program difficult to interpret. Evaluation of her program has suggested that different parent workers were differentially successful with parents in different Hawaiian communities. The one staff member whose parents were receptive and did keep their home visit appointments seemed "to serve a variety of functions to help the parents in all sorts of ways rather than applying solely the intended focus on the mother's role as teacher to reinforce a particular curriculum" (p. 25). A more narrowly didactic conception of the parent-worker role may not be effective despite conscientious efforts to train home workers in cognitive curriculum skills appropriate for a given child. *Process as well as content seems to be crucial in reaching and involving parents in the education of their children.*

Karnes, Hodgins, Teska, and Kirk (1969) tried to replicate their mother's group meeting program mentioned earlier with the extra provision of an enriched preschool for the children. The addition of a parent involvement component had no significant effect on children's scores if the children were enrolled in preschool.

In contrast to these findings, Sue Gray (1971) has reported encouraging results for mother participation plus child preschool experience. Three kinds of experience were provided. One group was provided with an enriched preschool and no parent involvement; one group had preschool with a carefully scheduled sequence of training experiences for mothers. These experiences were designed to enable mothers to work effectively with their young children and to take on some assistant teacher function in the preschool. The third group involved weekly home visitation and no preschool. Gray reports that "the IQ's of the group in which both mothers and children were involved in the preschool have tended to remain relatively stable . . . after the children have gone through their first two years of school. In the group in which the mothers were not involved, however, there has been a decrease in IQ"(p. 3).

Positive effects have also been reported in an experimental Head Start program of language intervention (Kuipers, Boger, and Beery 1970). Groups of mothers met in twelve weekly two-hour sessions with their children's teacher in a developmental language workshop, a structured language workshop, or in a placebo group workshop. At weekly orientations, a trainer would go over specifically prepared objectives, materials, and lessons with pairs of teachers. Weekly evaluation sessions were also held between trainers and teachers. Follow-up home visits allowed for provision of materials and directions to mothers unable to attend a meeting. Additionally, makeup lessons were provided at the school. Those mothers who participated in the specific language interaction groups increased their own language skills as well as the quality of interaction with their own children. Their children increased in language skills and also had a more positive perception of their mother's view of them in comparison to placebo treatment group children.

Boger and his colleagues (1974) have carried out an expansion and replication of this program with rural and urban parents. The major goal has been to increase and facilitate the social, affective, and language interactions of parents and children. The program also has developed an effective collegial model for trainer-teacher-parent interactions within an early childhood education setting. Helpful suggestions for enriching the process of parent-child interactions are included in the manual *Parents Are Teachers Too* (Boger, Kuipers, Wilson, and Andrews 1974).

Personnel decisions. When both preschool education and parent involving efforts are extensive and intensive activities of a project, decisions may have to be made about staff allocation. Some projects have separate personnel for these two activities. Other projects, such as Weikart's Perry Preschool Project in Ypsilanti have assigned teachers to preschool classrooms during mornings and these same teachers served as home visitor teachers during afternoons.

Parents in job-training; babies in comprehensive educational care. In Heber's program in Milwaukee (Heber, Garber, Harrington, Hoffman, and Falender 1972), the parent involvement component consisted of carefully sequenced and supervised on-the-job training experience as well as a great many parent group meetings to build self-confidence, communication skills, and job skills in a group of low IQ mothers from low-income households. The enrichment experiences for the children from earliest infancy to school age were intensive, and meticulously comprehensive in every area of child development. Extraordinary increases in the IQ scores (mean IQ=126) of the experimentally enriched children after four years in the program were found in comparison to declines in scores (mean IQ=95) of the control children. These results have made it very clear that even children from backgrounds of mothers with IQ's below 70 or 80 "are not doomed to inferiority by unalterable constraints either genetic or environmental" (Bronfenbrenner 1973, p. 54). It would be most difficult to assign a particular portion of these remarkable gains, however, to the very real and positive changes in job status and self-concept of the mothers, given the all-embracing and long-term nature of the program for the children from earliest infancy onward.

The parent involver as a catalyst. Infants and their mothers have been the focus of attempts to combine parent group meetings and developmental group care in an innovative effort at the Mt. Carmel Parent Child Center in Illinois. Earladeen Badger (1972)

25

launched an experimental Mother's Training Program there in addition to the ongoing Center program for infants. Prior to this special effort, the weekly meetings of mothers, organized and planned by social worker aides, had served mainly as social gatherings despite attempts by workers to provide lectures on child development and to introduce nutrition, crafts, health, and other topics.

Mothers then began to attend weekly two-hour instructional meetings with transportation plus care of other preschoolers provided. The group leader offered infant-toddler demonstrations, established a toy lending library, and made weekly follow-up visits to each home to offer individual help. Mothers became active in making play materials for their infants. Each mother learned to match toys with her own infant's developmental level. Monthly potluck suppers helped involve parents further with each other. Badger's conclusions express her conviction that a trainer's enthusiasm, belief in his or her own ability to effect change in poverty families, plus structure—such as a sequenced learning program—are indispensable ingredients to the success of parent involvement efforts. Not only the process of parent involving but who is carrying out this process may be critical for positive outcomes.

Badger has documented the caring and charismatic quality of her leadership in these parent group meetings in an impressive series of videotapes. The effects of this parent involvement program in infant education and development have been very promising. Early mastery of Piagetian sensorimotor skills by the infants in comparison with other infants, either home reared or reared in orphanages, has been reported (Hunt, Paraskevopoulos, Schickedanz, and Uzgiris 1974).

Parents as Teachers in Group Care Settings

Several variants of this model exist and some innovative directions are now being explored with this model.

Cooperative nurseries. Cooperative preschools have always involved parents—usually middle-socioeconomic class parents—in teaching roles as well as in planning and school management participation. Washington, D. C., for example, has had cooperative play programs for more than 31 years. Parent Cooperative Preschools International (1974) is an international council dedicated to strengthening the parent cooperative movement and helping communities to appreciate the importance of parent education for adults and preschool education for children.

26

Working with low-income parents, Bushell and Jacobsen (1968) have reported encouraging changes in maternal ability to use reinforcement techniques to shape and improve children's classroom behaviors. The mothers participating in the Juniper Gardens Cooperative Preschool were often on welfare and "barred from other forms of employment by deficits of education or experience" (p.11). The staff taught classroom management, planning group activities, establishment of interest areas, task analysis, and behavior modifications techniques to the mothers. The assumption was that "if Head Start-type programs can be operated by the parents of the children served, such programs will have a more noticeable impact on the community at large" (p. 2). An interesting portion of the training program involved teaching mothers the use of contingent praise rather than critical nagging. One mother was asked to coach another mother in how to tutor a child by tele-coaching—that is, by using a wireless microphone set in an open frequency. The mother-tutor wore an earphone connected to a pocket FM radio so she could receive feedback from the mother-coach for her attempts at positive reinforcement.

Family day care. Family day care parents, many with a child of their own, who use their own homes as day care centers for children of working parents, play an increasingly prominent role as teachers of young children in small groups. Social service personnel and day care mothers themselves unfortunately have often viewed the role as primarily a baby-sitting one (Emlen and Watson 1971). Active efforts are now underway to change this image (Sale and Torres 1971). A DARCEE program has been extensively involved in at-home training of family day care workers (Bridgman, Goodroe, Horton, Scanlan, and Strain 1971). DARCEE goals are to teach child development skills, and to help day care mothers to view their role as an educative agent.

Creative suggestions which could maximize the educational expertise of family day care homes have been offered by Lally (1972a) and by Nimnicht (1973). Envisioned is an early childhood education center which serves as a "wheel hub," a focal point in providing a broad range of community services and liaison functions for children and families. The functions could include provision of training personnel and toy- and book-lending services for day care homes within the service radius of the center.

The Family Day Care Training Project (1974) in Minneapolis represents an innovative effort to provide training for family and group day care parents. A variety of techniques to develop support systems are used. These include satellite resource centers, well-trained liaison consultants, field trips, toy workshops, a TV course, a radio course, and slide-tape presentations as well as University of Minnesota-based courses.

Foster parent care. Foster parents also have been trained to be more effective people with the children in their care. Foster Grandparent programs have been instituted in many communities. Grandparents often work with low socioeconomic status children and sometimes with retarded children. Thune (1970) has described the way in which foster grandparents (average age, 67 years old) in Nashville, Tennessee, were given ten weeks of training to develop their skills. Each foster grandparent helped a group of three nursery school children from low-income neighborhoods to learn within a trusting comfortable relationship with an older adult.

The Parent Effectiveness Training Program (PET) developed by Gordon (Thompson and Patrick 1970) teaches foster parents communication skills through role-playing, practice, and lectures. Parents learn to listen actively to what a child is trying to communicate about his or her problems, to communicate personal feelings—"I" messages—when a problem is the parent's and not the child's, and to resolve conflicts by mutual active working out of solutions by children and parents.

Project Follow Through: Parents as volunteers and aides in elementary school. One of the 21 Follow-Through planned variations in elementary education combines home visitation with parent classroom participation. This approach

> emphasizes the tie between teacher and parent as co-educators of the children. Home visitors regularly teach parents of kindergarten, first, second and third grade children how to help their child's development. The visitors coordinate the educational help the parents give their children with the child's classroom activities. Parents are encouraged to spend considerable time in the classroom as volunteers and aides. Teachers meet often with parents to learn from them about the child and to work out shared activities to foster the child's education. . . . Parents whose children participate in |this] approach are more satisfied with their children's education and more optimistic about the value of education. (Datta 1973, p. 28)

The communications system for implementing this program involves a liaison officer for each community. Videotapes of the home learning tasks developed by teachers and parent educators in each community are sent to the University each week. The project also used videotapes creatively in the training of parent educators to help them identify specific desirable teaching behaviors to be used when presenting tasks to parents (Gordon, Greenwood, Ware, and Olmsted 1974; Gordon et al. 1979).

Teachers serve as models for mothers in group settings. The Sumner Mobile Preschool Program in Syracuse, New York (Greenstein, Garman, and Sanford 1974), is another program which trains mothers in the home while it provides a developmental program for young children. In this program, trained teachers transport preschoolers, whose older siblings all attend the same neighborhood school, to a mother's home two or three mornings a week. There a teacher serves as a model for such behaviors as: use of snacktime to teach shapes and colors (of plates and utensils), counting (of napkins), taking turns, and other competencies. The parent gradually takes on a variety of program responsibilities such as planning cooking experiences, story reading, and other activities both with her own children and with those who attend the mobile preschool in her home.

Gordon and Guinagh's (1969) backyard centers have used somewhat the same concept. Mothers in whose homes preschool activities occurred for a small group of children were employed as helpers to the backyard center directors. These directors themselves were paraprofessionals who had served earlier as teachers in Gordon's home visitation program. While the child was in the program, a parent educator worked once a week with the mother, who was instructed not only in the mechanics of Piagetian-based games and tasks, but also "in general attitudes toward them, and some conceptual frameworks and rationale for their use. The essential mode of presentation is demonstration by the parent educator and modeling by the mother" (p. 7).

This trend toward helping parents and trainees to become early childhood personnel through the use of trained staff as models in actual work situations has been accelerated by the newly funded Child Development Associate (CDA) program. The CDA program (1973) will certify competence gained predominantly through supervised experience in an actual child care center rather than by formal training.

Hiring parents just because they are parents. Many programs make an effort to hire parents of children enrolled in programs. It is essential to respect the cultural background of children in fostering their development and such hiring practices are one way of implementing this respect.

> It is important to try not to change people's culture, but to make children familiar with many cultures. Foods,

songs, games, languages, staff, clothes, sleeping patterns, holiday celebrations, and all other customs
should reflect the cultural background of the children
and parents being served. This is central to the socialization of all children. It is intellectually enriching and
emotionally fulfilling. (Lally 1970, p. 6)

Yet a note of caution should be sounded about programs
which hire parents in order to foster and enhance respect for the
child's cultural background, but provide little or no preservice and
in-service training, and still expect that optimal caregiving will result.
Supports must be made available to any child care staff personnel.
The importance of the selection of people with bilingual strengths,
cultural appropriateness, and parenthood status may be vitiated unless their selection is coupled with active and continuous training. If
such training is provided then this caution may not apply. Indeed,
under optimal selection and training procedures the choice of paraprofessionals can be singularly enriching not only for the children in a
program but for the professional staff as well (Lally, Honig, and Caldwell 1973).

Forced parent participation in group care. Another special caution must be sounded about forced participation of parents in
child care programs. Parents have sometimes been required to serve
in the classroom as a condition for the provision of care for their
children. Programs which attempt to "force" parents as a condition
of the acceptance of children to participate as regular observers, volunteers, or workers in early education settings may run into some
special difficulties. A mother may feel she needs predominantly the
child care aspect of even the most developmentally enriching program
so that she herself can finish schooling, learn a profession, or work to
support the child. Some mothers are "at-home" mothers, but perhaps
only through lengthy development of a trusting relationship with program personnel and many contacts with child development ideas in
action can they come to understand and to value developmental day
care for their children and themselves. Categorically enforcing a condition of frequent attendance in the classroom for low-income or
low-education parents may vitiate program goals, since families who
need programs the most may not initially be prepared to fulfill lengthy
or stringent criteria of center visits or participation.

Johnson (1973) has reported notable success at involving
parents in classrooms with their children when such efforts were
made in the *second* year of the program after an initial year of home
visitation with parents. Cultural mores among the Mexican-American

30

families served by this project would have made such participation much more improbable if it had been required of families early in the project.

    Gradual movement to classroom participation. Horton (n.d.) at DARCEE has described a program where classroom participation is the final step in a training program for mothers which first involves orientation and directed observation, then demonstration and role-play, then classroom participation with limited responsibility, and finally classroom participation with instructional responsibility as permanent assistants. This graduated process may prove feasible in solving the problems of encouraging parent participation in the classroom while ensuring effectiveness of functioning.

Television Aids to Parent Involvement in Children's Learning

    "Sesame Street" is probably the best known television program designed to facilitate early learning. "The Electric Company" television programs have aimed at improving young children's reading skills.

    Sprigle (1972) has made serious criticisms of television programs per se as inexpensive educational boosters for poverty children.

> When one strips away the colorful image-making in Sesame Street programs and takes a close look at the substance, one finds that education is sacrificed for entertainment. The mere manipulation of alphabet letters and numbers does not make a program educational. . . .
>
> An educational program for poverty children stands or falls on the arrangements made for enhancing developmental status, for timing and continuity of learning steps, sound methods of teaching and learning considering individual differences in ability and mode of learning. Its success depends on the typing together of learning with the emotional, social, motivational and attitudinal aspects of the poverty child's development. . . .
>
> . . . there is a definite message: there are simply no short cuts through the problems of educating proverty children. This heightened awareness of the complexity and enormity of the problem of educating the poverty child is at once a challenge, an opportunity and a danger. It is a challenge because many of us have tried but a solution to the problem remains elusive. It is an opportunity because, if educators, researchers, and government will

31

use these findings constructively, a number of desirable outcomes could flow. And, it is a danger because Sesame Street and other programs with surface appearances of education may be thrust at the public as easy answers to a complicated problem. (pp. 108-109)

In contrast, some television programs are used as an important component of an early education program involving parents. In Appalachia, the Home-Oriented Preschool Education (HOPE) program (Alford 1972) has used 30-minute five-day-a-week televised lessons called "Around the Bend" as a springboard to encourage young children from three to five years of age to want to learn. HOPE instructs parents through a home visitation program in ways to use these special television programs so that positive parent-child interactions are promoted and parents can become effective teachers with their children. The outlay and operating costs quoted are about $270 per child per year. A home visitor once a week delivers Parent Guides to television activities and provides materials for parent and child to use together. Additionally the home visitor carries out some learning activity with the family. A mobile preschool comes to the community several half-days per week so that children also have a chance for group experiences with a preschool teacher who coordinates the group's activities with home and television activities.

The "Sesame Street" program is similarly used as a resource by home visitors for involving parents in their children's learning careers in the Dilenowisco Early Childhood Development program (1973). This program within the Appalachian region also provides an education stimulation unit working in the home with mothers of children six to thirty months of age who might have possible learning deficiencies.

In 1978, Bob Keeshan introduced the use of "Picturepages" into his "Captain Kangaroo" TV program. These materials are designed to involve parents with their preschool children's development.

Home Start plus television. In the rugged Appalachian mountain area of Tennessee served by a Home Start program

social and other services are limited. Most families have a low educational level, generally less than the eighth grade; and yet, in spite of the poverty, 95 percent of the families have television sets. This preponderance of television led the Home Start program to focus on educational television as one of its major educational components. In addition to television the program uses home visits for parents and children, and a teacher who works with small groups of children in a mobile-van classroom. The television component is based on the *Captain Kangaroo* program, and weekly supportive activity guides for parents and home visitors are published to supplement the daily television program's activities. These guides, which are distributed to a variety of people nationwide, list different activities that can be easily done each day in a home setting, and feature home-made materials. The mobile classroom, which provides a weekly group activity for children (especially important in such a rural area where families often live miles apart), is equipped with desks, tables, puzzles, games, filmstrips, records, and toys. Parents sometimes assist the teachers on a volunteer basis and are welcome to visit while their children attend classes. (O'Keefe 1973b, p.27)

Such programs use television as a valuable tool for teaching and as a valued partner in enlisting and focusing parental interest in a preschool child's learning career. Television teaching without such a boost from parents may not produce long-lasting cognitive achievements.

Omnibus Programs

These are programs which use a wide variety of techniques and carry out long-term parent involvement efforts often extending from prenatal through school years. For example, the Kentucky Rural Child Care Project (1972) is dedicated to "total involvement of the family unit from birth to school age" (p. 1). Prenatal checkups provided in this project assure the child a head start even before birth. Later on, a Parent-Child Center (PCC) offers education to the young infant.

From the time of birth, an Infant Educator visits the home weekly to aid the mother in all aspects of infant care. From three months until two years, the child comes with his mother once a week to a brightly decorated well-equipped infant room, for educational activities. When he is two years old, the PCC child attends the center alone one day a week, for a full day of activities. On another day his mother comes along, and they work and play together, guided by the Infant Educator.

All this is for the small child. For his parents there is medical care, including counseling when necessary, and general instruction about such family concerns as nutrition, child development, and budgeting. For the mothers, sewing and craft work are taught in the afternoons during the child's naptime; for the dads, there are wood-working and craft classes at the center's workshop; night classes on various subjects are offered to them and other interested persons from the community.

Also for the parents are six salaried staff positions, paid from a Parent Participation Fund. In addition, both PCC and Head Start parents work one week a year, as aides paid minimum wages. On one other day each month the parents from Head Start groups must volunteer for duties at the center. (Kentucky Rural Child Care Project 1972, p. 1)

The Family Development Research Program in Syracuse, New York, offers another omnibus approach to parent involvement (Lally 1972b, 1973; Lally and Honig 1975b). Paraprofessional home visitors, who are indigenous to the low-income community they serve, bring nutritional, child development, and child care information to pregnant mothers. After the infant's birth, the family is taught special games to encourage visual alerting, eye-hand coordinations, and vocalizations. Mothers are encouraged to breast-feed and to improve their own and their baby's diets. At six months, infants enter the Children's Center, a developmental day care program. Families continue to be visited by the Child Development Trainers (CDTs), and parents continue to receive child development information and skills until the child reaches school age. Language, sensorimotor, and later preoperational games and tasks are presented as well as child-management ideas and techniques. CDTs lend toys and books. They provide information and references to community resources to help with legal aid, health care, housing, food stamps, and other problems. They provide loyal friendships to mothers often beset with severe emotional, sexual, social, and financial crises. This function was poignantly corroborated by mothers during the Parent Evaluation Interview administered when the child is three years old. Asked what made the home visitor effective, mothers answered that they considered the home visitor a friend who became involved with and seemed to care about them as well as their child, and who always showed up on time no matter how derelict the mother was in keeping appointments, or how mistrusting or uninterested the mother had acted for a long time.

CDTs serve as liaison persons between the parent and the center. Complaint department, information clearing house about center activities, escort service for parents visiting the center, participant in parent group monthly discussion meetings, active worker at weekly parent workshops, bearer of special family news a teacher may need to know—all these are roles filled by the CDT as his or her repertoire of family-facilitating skills expands. CDTs hold parent group meetings in homes for those parents who are interested in group discussions of and films about special topics. Topics which parents have requested include: effective parent participation in the public school after the child enters the school, sexuality and early childhood, and working mothers and young children.

It is often impossible to determine what portion of this home visitor repertoire may be the catalyst for a particular family's increasing positive involvement with a child's growth and learning. *The ultimate effectiveness of parent involvers may depend on their flexible ability to serve a multitude of functions in families with a multitude of problems.*

Lally's program gives particular attention to the importance of selection, preservice, and in-service training of the home visitors. The paraprofessionals initially underwent eight weeks of training in nutrition, health, interviewing techniques, and games and activities to facilitate early cognitive development. Dietitians, child psychologists, sociologists, nurses, and teachers each demonstrated skills from their own fields which would help make home visits more useful to and more successful with parents. A variety of training techniques were used. In addition to lectures and talks, the trainees had practice and role-playing sessions which gave practical experience in necessary skills as well as insights into potential problems. Several weeks were spent working in the classroom with infants and their teachers.

In-service training has included workshops to increase knowledge base and special skills in working with families as children grow older. Sharing strategies to help families with an ever-widening array of problems is also part of the weekly in-service sessions. Lally and Honig (1974a) report:

> We have learned over the last five years that some of the basic needs and fears must be met head-on and not buried under pages of games and tasks for a mother and her child. . . . [There is a] complex interaction of personal, social, and economic variables that affect the day-to-day functioning of our families. . . . Families are motivated by many factors that must be taken into consideration by outside agents if they expect to have a meaningful impact on family functioning. We have learned one lesson well. No one program structure works for everyone. A program must be dynamic, fluid and attuned to the needs of the individuals who are served. (pp. 13-15)

This project has also produced a handbook designed to teach caregivers how to facilitate the education and development of children under three (Honig and Lally 1972).

Models That Bridge: Early Childhood into Elementary School Years*

Some recent innovations have involved supports for families and children that do not cease as soon as the child leaves the preschool years. One of the most comprehensive program efforts to involve families of preschoolers in enhancing living and learning conditions for their children is Child and Family Resource Program (CFRP), a national Head Start demonstration program, which was initially funded in June 1973. CFRP uses Head Start as a base for developing a community wide service delivery network.

> The CFRP process begins with the enrollment of the family, which is followed by an assessment of the needs and strengths of the family unit. On the basis of discussions between family members, CFRP staff, and community resource specialists, the unique goals and needs of each family are assessed, and ways are discussed in which both the family and CFRP staff can contribute to an overall Family Action Plan for meeting identified needs. (O'Keefe 1978, p. 1)

A key feature of CFRP programs is flexibility and thoroughness in meeting family and child needs. This individualization and tailoring of programs to fit each family is a strength that augurs well for the success of CFRP programs. Most research and demonstration models funded earlier could only take families willing to fit the model of that particular program. Now there is a federal model to fit families.

Another excellent feature of CFRP programs is the attempt to link resources in each community to serve the diagnostic and remediation needs of family members. A third admirable feature of this program is the provision of continuity of services from the prenatal period through early elementary school years. Unfortunately, funding of many other projects with excellent preschool curricular and parent involvement efforts has often abruptly stopped when the child entered elementary school. Some families require continuity of service. Some

*This section is adapted from "Working with Parents of Preschool Children" by A. S. Honig. In *Parent Education and Intervention Handbook,* edited by R. Abidin, 1980. Courtesy of Charles C. Thomas, Publishers, Springfield, Illinois.

children and some school systems may find their adjustment to one another far better where CFRP personnel help provide continuity of care and continuity of resources should they be needed by an individual family. The fourth objective of CFRP is to enhance and build upon the strengths of the individual family as a childrearing system with distinct values, culture, and aspirations.

Community Institutions and Parent Involvement in Child Care

Churches and temples. Many religious institutions currently provide facilities for early child care programs. Some also attempt to provide families with help for parent-child conflicts and communication difficulties. A church bulletin board notice the author recently noted on the door of an after-school care program read, "If you and your child are having troubles with each other come and see someone at our family counseling service."

Hospitals and clinics. In St. Paul, Minnesota, the Children's Hospital sends a "toy lady" every week to bring ideas and encouragement to parents of young patients. The goal of improving early learning and emotional development is also furthered by the outpatient clinic, since "parents can bring their children's school or discipline problems as well as their sore throats" (Office of Child Development 1973, p.26).

In Los Angeles, the John Tracy Clinic (1968) for deaf children provides parents with guides toward helping language development. These easy-to-read lesson plans for parents are a good source of ideas for boosting a child's language development within the home setting and the boundaries of ordinary daily activities.

Community resources: an antidote to scarce funding. Funds for large-scale research programs in early child care and parent involvement have become increasingly scarce. Perhaps we should more vigorously and creatively utilize community organizations, long accepted in neighborhoods, as resources which can expand their services to include helping parents find ways to better living and learning with and for their children. Community storefront walk-in services for helping citizens with rent or employment problems might serve as scattered-site headquarters for toy lending libraries, as resource centers for films and literature on how children grow, and as part-time consulting centers for helping parents with ideas and techniques for childrearing and educating.

Self-help and community methods of parent involvement. Many parents have begun parent-to-parent community-based groups to help each other learn more about parenting. In a Syracuse, New York program, each parent-to-parent meeting includes a brief presentation by a parent on some basic aspect of parenting, refreshments, experience-sharing, and discussion. This program is a volunteer grassroots effort by parents to involve themselves more knowledgeably in their babies' growth and development.

Hot line programs for parents are becoming available in some communities. These may be adjuncts to pediatric clinics or child abuse programs. In Los Angeles, the Cedars-Sinai Medical Center has a telephone counseling service for "normal parents with normal worries" called Warm Line (Reid 1977, p. 664). Pediatric services are beginning to be used as settings for parent involvement activities (Honig 1979c; Jackson and Terdal 1978; Morris 1974).

In Seattle, Washington, Stett (Richard 1978) founded the Parent Place, an agency that offers help with parenting problems in classes and counseling sessions. The agency has a Parent Panic Line, a telephone crisis number for parents who need immediate help.

Somewhat more formal networks are organized in some states to coordinate separate services. Programs in Ohio that provide services for infants (birth through age three) have recently organized into a council called United Services for Effective Parenting (Burns 1978).

More commercial efforts to provide information and assistance are also available in innovative forms. The Young Parents Book Club (Stamford, CT 06904) provides access to publications on parent involvement and early childrearing. Burton White's (1979) Center for Parent Education in Newton, Massachusetts, was recently founded to provide information and support for parents. The Profession of Parenting Institute (Brodsky n.d.) has been established in Philadelphia to teach parenting skills and to organize parents for political activism. Two workbooks are available from the Institute.

Models Directed to Parents in Alternate Lifestyles

Many resources and materials have become available in the past few years for the very young parent, the teenager who will soon become a parent, divorced and single parents, parents in other than two-parent nuclear parenting situations, and multiproblem families.

Young parents. Just as prevention is considered preferable to cure, so should efforts be made to ensure parenting skills before young people become parents. Such programs need to include

38

family life education and sex education components to increase awareness of all the ramifications of responsible parenting as well as meeting current developmental needs of the teenagers. Audiovisual materials, some of which are noted in the Resources section, are becoming increasingly available to facilitate such programs.

Education for Parenthood Programs. Programs which focus on teaching teens parenting skills have been launched nationally (Kruger 1973). A joint grant from the Office of Child Development and the Office of Education to the Education Development Corporation is assisting in the development of curricular materials and methods for parenthood education among teenagers in public schools. Among the approaches recommended are the following:

> The use of a child development laboratory or other field site practicum so that students can observe children's behavior and assess the value of different techniques used by adults in child care activities.
>
> The use of film strips and audio cassettes, which enables the instructor to bring a variety of case studies into the classroom.
>
> Encouragement of group discussion, which often centers around problems experienced by the students in their laboratory assignments.
>
> The use of such instruments of observation as rating scales and check-lists to help the students analyze what is happening within situations involving young children, so they will understand why certain behaviors are exhibited and see how they might be modified. (p. 7)

Consortium on early childbearing and rearing. Another important parent involvement effort was directed toward teenagers who are already parents (Nelson 1973). Through dissemination of research (Williams 1972, 1974), conferences, workshops, and a regularly published journal, *Sharing,* the Consortium on Early Childbearing and Childrearing contributed knowledge to and about positive programs which are being introduced by communities across the country to meet the needs of teenage parents and their infants. Cooper (1974) developed a parenting curriculum for school-age parents for the Consortium. Due to limited federal funding, the Consortium has been phased out as of March 31, 1975; however, the publications are available from the Child Welfare League of America, 67 Irving Place, New York, NY 10003.

National organizations such as the Future Homemakers of America (1977) and the Salvation Army (MacLachlan and Cole 1978) have created and carried out parenting curricula with young parents.

Some programmatic efforts combine models and goals in innovative ways. In the Parent Readiness Education Project (PREP), sponsored by the United States Office of Education, parents observe their children in a classroom and receive activities to do daily at home with their children. Parents also meet in groups to discuss topics relating to raising and nurturing children. A special focus of PREP is to help high school students learn about parenting and child development.

One of the most well-known of the efforts to teach child development and parenting to junior and senior high school students is the Exploring Early Childhood Program (Felt 1978). Students learn about child development and themselves while working closely and regularly with young children (Jones 1975).

Fathers and parenting. Fathers as parent involvers are receiving an increasing share of national attention, whether they are functioning in two-parent or single-parent families (Bartz and Witcher 1978; Biller and Meredith 1974; Clarke-Stewart 1977b; Dodson 1974; Honig 1978a; Lamb 1975, 1976; Lynn 1974; McAdoo 1979; McCall and Young 1979; Pannor et al. 1971; Santrock 1970, 1975; Schlesinger 1978).

Parent involvement in families with divorce. Stresses have been increasing in families, whether from breakup of parents or from a variety of personal, social, and economic problems. More support systems are needed to help parents be positively involved with children under these new family conditions that often lead to stress and difficulty for children (DHEW 1974a; Duncan and Duncan 1979; Gardner 1970; Grollman 1969; Hetherington and Deur 1971; Hetherington et al. 1978a, 1978b, 1978c; Hoffman 1971; Horejsi 1979; S. Jenkins 1978; O'Keefe 1978; Riddle 1977; Stuart and Abt 1972; Tuckman and Regan 1966; Wheelock College 1978).

Other lifestyles. A variety of other alternate lifestyles and programs to serve these families' needs are considered in Curtis 1976; Eiduson 1978, n.d.; Eiduson and Alexander 1978; Goodman 1977; Harrell and Pizzo 1973; Honig 1979a; Klein 1974; Morin and Schultz 1978; and issues of *The Single Parent* published by Parents without Partners. Many films about families in alternate lifestyles or under stress are available through Polymorph Films (1978).

40

Parent Involvement and Children at Risk Developmentally

As we increase our skills in saving infants at birth, more infants are at risk with mental, physical, and emotional handicaps. Parental skills and involvement in their child's development have been found to be especially crucial for optimizing the chances for such children (Willerman et al. 1970).

The Wisconsin Portage Project utilizes home teachers to provide parents with activities for multihandicapped preschoolers (Shearer and Shearer 1972).

Public Law 94–142, The Education for All Handicapped Children Act, came into effect in 1975. The law mandates a written individualized education program (IEP) for each handicapped child who requires special programming. This law has spurred the creation of programs and materials, many of them aimed at parents. For example. *The Exceptional Parent* magazine provides specific information to help parents of exceptional children. See articles by Bassin and Drovetta (1976) or the glowing tribute paid by severely physically handicapped (and college graduate) Terry Haffner (1976) to his parents' involvement in his flourishing development.

Teaching Exceptional Children contains articles such as Kroth's (1978) "Parents—Powerful and Necessary Allies." The journal *Children Today* often provides useful program ideas for working with parents of handicapped children (Hosey 1973; Hutinger and McKee 1979; Jew 1974; Magnus 1974; Levenson et al. 1978).

Many organizations provide specialized materials for parents whose children have *specific* handicaps. The Ohio Resource Center for the Visually Handicapped provides a bibliography of resources for parents (Armstrong et al. 1978). Head Start (1976) publishes a bibliography of resources for parents of preschool handicapped children. So does the Bureau of Education for the Handicapped (Cadman et al. 1976). State departments of education often publish such materials (Florida Department of Education 1975; R.A. Smith 1977; Sumpter and Metger 1977).

Rising child abuse rates underscore the urgency of political and legislative efforts to provide funds for *preventative* programs aimed at preparing young people for responsible and freely chosen entry into the world of parenting (DHEW 1977a). The extent and consequences of school-age parenting are documented by several research studies (Furstenberg 1976; Oppel and Royston 1971; Parker and Kleiner 1966; Whelan and Higgins 1973).

De Lissovoy (1973) has documented poignantly how a lack of knowledge of normal child developmental milestones plus socioeconomic stresses of poverty and lack of education can result in young parents' unrealistic expectations for babies and children. Punitive, insensitive, and inappropriate parenting styles may then become all too frequent.

Descriptions of services offered to young and single parents are available from several projects: Bracken 1971; Danforth et al. 1971; Heger 1977; Middleman 1970; Packer, Resnick, Resnick, and Wilson 1979; Zitner and Hayden 1979.

More resources are also available to professionals involved in services to young parents (Dreskin 1978; Gordon and Wollin 1975; Grow 1979; Honig 1978b; Howard 1975a, 1975b; Levenson et al. 1978; National Federation of Settlements and Neighborhood Centers 1976; Nelson 1973; *Teen Times* 1977). Parents' Magazine Films (1978) has produced a series of four sound and color filmstrips entitled "The School-Age Parent."

These and other materials are urgently needed as the number of teenage parents has consistently risen during the past decade.

State Departments of Health also provide materials. The Arkansas Department of Health distributes a delightful pamphlet "Will Your Baby Learn to Read?" to parents who bring infants to health clinics (Haney 1978).

Other publications and materials for helping parents with children at risk developmentally are Badger 1977; Burns 1978; Cansler et al. 1976; Christopherson et al. 1976; Concept Media 1977; J.O. Cooper 1978; Daniel and Hyde 1975; Drouillard and Raynor 1977; L. Fraser 1973; Golden and Davis 1974; S. Gordon 1975; Honig 1979a; Instructional Materials Center n.d.; Johnson and Werner 1975; Jones 1977; Kroth 1975, 1978; Levitt and Cohen 1977; Lillie et al. n.d.; Marx 1972; Mills 1976; Offir 1976; Perske 1973; Raifner and Drouillard 1975; Sitnick et al. n.d.; Stewart 1978; Swirsky 1977; Turnbull and Turnbull 1978; DHEW 1977; Weigerink 1979.

Parent Involvement in Child Care Through Participation in Political Power Organizations

Voice for Children, the monthly publication of the Day Care and Child Development Council of America, ran a banner headline "1500 Assert Parent Power" (1972, p.1). The headline referred to

42

the emergence of the National Parents Federation for Day Care and Child Development as a leading force in the establishment of a national organization which belongs to parents. This organization promotes the rights of parents to increased involvement and to "direct communication to parents in local, state, and regional affairs involving child care" (p. 2), through community and political work. The National Parents Federation has asked for recognition by the federal government as the representative of concerned parents of children in child care programs across the United States.

Parent power in the political arena will probably increase of necessity as long as political priority systems undervalue and undersupport programs which emphasize effective parenting skills, developmental day care, and child care services in general. Political efforts by parents to increase legislative appropriations for developmental services to children express a vital commitment to optimal child development and education. Lois-Ellen Datta (1973) has aptly remarked that "parent involvement as a philosophy is consistent with the political system of participatory democracy" (p. 68).

Childrearing and public policy. Several new publications are now available to encourage advocacy on behalf of children. Among these are Beck 1979; Brodsky n.d.; Bronfenbrenner 1974, 1975; Callahan 1973; Clarke-Stewart 1977a; Gallagher et al. 1979; General Accounting Office 1979; Hogan and Schwartz 1979; Keniston 1977; National Academy of Sciences 1976; National Clearinghouse for Home-Based Services to Children 1979; PMIC 1977; SRCD 1979; Talbot 1976; Vaughan and Brazelton 1976.

4

Evaluation Problems and Practices in Parent Involvement

As indicated earlier with regard to specific models and projects surveyed, some difficult problems are involved in assessing the effectiveness of parent involvement efforts upon the performance and achievements of children in a family. But assessment problems also exist with respect to goals for parents. For their own growth, parents need to find more pleasure and pride and sense of doing an important and well-done job in the raising of their children and in taking care of their own needs for training, for work, for effective social interactions. Parents need to learn to articulate their own needs and goals—for themselves and for their children—and to feel that things can be different in their lives despite possible poverty or educational lacks. Global and multidimensional attitudes and behaviors involved in the pursuance of these goals do not easily lend themselves to measurement.

Child Change as a Function of Parent Involvement

Changes in children as a function of parent involvement in their learning have been assessed by a variety of measures. Some programs utilize direct child assessments; others use parent and/or teacher ratings.

Cognitive achievements have been assessed by Piagetian measures, by preschool achievement tests, such as the Caldwell-Soule Preschool Inventory (Caldwell 1970), the Wide Range Achievement Test, or the Metropolitan Reading Readiness Test, as well as language tests such as the Illinois Test of Psycholinguistic Abilities, and standard IQ tests. Social-emotional functioning and achievement motivation of children in combined child care and parent involvement programs is frequently assessed by means of observed and rated classroom interactions with peers, adults, and tasks or by means of teacher ratings (Beller 1969; Emmerich 1971; Honig, Caldwell, and Tannenbaum 1970; Schaefer n.d.).

The Syracuse University Family Development Research program (Lally 1974) has recently begun to interview mothers after they and their children have participated in a home visit plus day care program for at least two-and-one-half years. Mothers are asked to contrast the target child's standing in comparison with siblings and peers, on intellective and social behaviors which are program goals. Preliminary data indicate that families in the program see their children in comparison with siblings as more sharing, more self-assertive, less shy, more likely to ask questions, make their own choices, and teach other children. Peer comparisons additionally showed that program children were perceived as more often trying new and difficult tasks and doing much less fighting.

Who Benefits Most From Parent Involvement?

In the DARCEE program, parent involvement, whether by means of mothers' meetings additional to preschool or through home visits only, did not produce significant effects on target children's scores. Participation, however, was associated with significantly superior Stanford-Binet scores of the *younger* siblings of the target children compared to DARCEE preschool only or no-treatment comparison groups (Gilmer, Miller, and Gray 1970). Where to measure the impact of parent-involvement efforts—with target children, with parents themselves, or with younger or older siblings—may be a difficult but important issue to decide.

When Do Parent Involvement Effects Show Up?

Radin (1972) carried out a program of multiple educational inputs in order to discover the contribution of differential amounts of parent participation to program effectiveness. In her program, eighty four-year-old children from low-income homes were enrolled for a full year in a half-day, four-day-a-week preschool program.

Group I children received supplemental biweekly tutoring from teachers with no parental involvement. Children in Group II were tutored with mothers present and involved. Mothers of Group III children, in addition to their attendance during home tutorial work, participated in small group discussions about childrearing. Group III was considered the "maximal" parent involvement group. Pre- and post-program measures of child IQ and of maternal attitudes toward childrearing and cognitive stimulation in the home were administered. All children gained significantly. That is, the "maximal" involvement of parents (as defined by home tutorial work with mother present plus parent group meetings) produced no discernable differences in children at the end of the one-year program. However, a limited follow-up study one year after program termination indicated that children from the "maximal" parent involvement group just described achieved the highest scores compared to contrast children whose parents had lesser or no program involvement. Additionally, the most clearly desirable maternal attitude changes were found in the group of mothers offered such maximum participation. Thus not only *where* to look for parent involvement but *when* may need to be considered in program planning. Longitudinal designs can be more costly but may be indispensable to clarify the effectiveness of different degrees and kinds of parent involvement efforts.

Motivation Issues in Parent Involvement Evaluation

When parents are willing to participate in long-term group or home-visit intervention projects, then their motivation to improve children's learning may be impressively different from that of control parents who have not so participated. Such differences could result in very different interpretations of the effectiveness of parent involvement programs. For example, a parent who agrees to place an infant in a developmental care project setting prior to six months may be different in complex ways from a control group parent who would have refused to place the baby in a day care setting at so young an age. As Honig (1972) has noted, such differences in parental feelings and attitudes may affect subsequent infant development more than a particular teaching practice or program curriculum whose effects on parent and child are being evaluated. Measured differences may be more difficult to interpret.

Some programs have been aware of the potential effects which differing maternal motivation could possibly exert. These programs have tried to find ways to ascertain whether maternal motivation is or is not a relevant variable accounting for positive effects among children. Karnes, Teska, Hodgins, and Badger (1970) tried to assess the effect of maternal motivational variables on child IQ measures in a 15-month education program for low-income mothers of infants and toddlers. Large IQ differences were found between the target child in the family and a sibling control. These differences were even greater than the IQ advantages which were achieved by target children in comparison to nonsibling controls. Thus target child gains could be attributed to the parent program per se rather than to any motivational differences.

Focus on Parent Growth As Well As Child Development

Since parents are a child's most important people, and his or her earliest and most continuous teachers, more and more attention has been given not only to possible child gains over the relatively short life span of enrichment programs but to increases in positive maternal attitudes and competencies with respect to self development as well as child development.

The Nurseries in Cross-Cultural Education (NICE) program for children and parents in San Francisco (Lane, Elzey, and Lewis 1971) has searched actively for varieties of experiences by which parents of children in a multicultural preschool can become more involved with their children's learning and with their own growth and development as adults. Their program has documented and emphasized some of the changes in parents themselves as they were helped by teachers, social workers, and each other. Parents participated in a variety of ways—brown-bag lunches at the preschool, informal parent education groups, and, finally, a series of two-hour parent training classes for fifteen weeks. The parents spent one day a week at the nursery school trying out ideas discussed in class. Parents were encouraged to share their own childhood experiences with each other and to help determine some of the course content. The parents, through observing and writing about their own, their child's, and other children's experiences and feelings, came to have a great deal more understanding of developmental problems and confidence in their own resources as reflected in home visit ratings and parents' own written descriptions.

48

Measuring Parent Change

A difficult problem in assessing parent involvement program effects is that often what the worker attempts to change is a parent's feelings of self-worth, sense of competency, self-help skills, sense of involvement in community actions to improve minority or poverty conditions.

Adequate measures of parent self-worth are in short supply, and even when some attitude measures are found, they may not be considered acceptable by parents participating in a given program.

Behaviors may well prove easier to observe or inquire about than attitudes. Some behaviors may also prove to be good indicators of parental changes in self-esteem, trust, parenting skills, and earlier and more positive acceptance of educational values for the child. It should be recognized, however, that if life conditions are difficult, whether due to minority status, poverty, or personal stresses, then movement toward some specific behavioral goals could occur, yet it might not mean that a parent would "succeed." Societal and personal injustices and difficulties can turn a parent's struggle and movement toward success into one more frustrating condition. Most parent education programs cannot largely affect broader social conditions of poverty and racism.

Below are listed behaviors which some programs consider helpful in understanding movement toward parental involvement in early childhood education program goals.

1. Parent is mostly at home when a program worker comes for a scheduled visit.

2. Parents visit and/or take an active part in a child's care center or school. (This measure may not be a fair one, since a parent may not be able to come because of schooling and job obligations. Evening or weekend participation in a parent group or in Open School Night, for example, may be a better index.)

3. Parent returns to school to get a high school or equivalency diploma or to obtain further education or to get job training.

4. Parent takes a child to different places—supermarket, zoo, park, visiting a neighbor.

5. Parent gets a job in order to provide for the child the things he or she thinks the child needs.

6. Parent effectively carries out a program game with a baby or child during a home visit so that the home visitor easily judges that the parent has worked with the child on a task or activity left in the home during the preceding week.

7. A mother's ability to maintain a more lasting relationship with a man, regardless of marital status, increases the possibility that a more stable father figure is available for the child.

8. Parents in a parent involvement program promote the advantages of the program to the point that neighbors and friends telephone to ask whether their children can be admitted. Parents may also bring relatives, (male and female) friends, and neighbors to any open group meeting the program offers. In a home-based program, neighbors may telephone to ask if they can be visited too.

9. Parent uses more alternative discipline methods and more positive methods. Mothers, for example, may continue to scold, but also begin to use more praise with the child and, additionally, now offer some kind of reason or explanation along with "yelling at the child."

These changes may be assessed by means of interviews with parents using schedules such as the Parent Inventory (Schaefer and Aronson n.d.), the Maternal Behavior Research Instrument (Schaefer and Bell 1958), the Caldwell and Honig (1965) Implicit Parental Learning Theory Inventory (IPLET),[2] and the Cognitive Home Environment Scale (Weikart, Deloria, Lawser, and Weigerink 1970), instruments designed to measure attitude and behavorial change techniques of parents.

> 10. Childbearing rate slows or halts until mother feels she has education and/or job security to provide for more children.
>
> 11. Parent reports spending more time with child.
>
> 12. More cognitive stimulation is offered in the home.

One extensively used measure of such changes is Caldwell's observation and interview measure, Inventory of Home Stimulation (STIM) (Caldwell and Richmond 1967). STIM surveys aspects of the home environment such as orderliness, safe play conditions, and books in the home. Wachs, Uzgiris, and Hunt (1971), using a modified version of this interview, found that several parental items related to a child's cognitive development during the first two years. These items were:

> There is at least one magazine placed where the child could play with it or look at it; the child was given regular training in one or more skills; the mother spontaneously vocalizes to the child; the mother spontaneously names at least one object to the child while the observer is in the home; the father helped take care of the child; the father played with the child at least ten minutes a day, the child is regularly spoken to by parents during mealtimes. (pp. 295-304)

---

2. IPLET comes in versions for five age groups. Each IPLET for the first four age groups consists of 45 items. Parents are asked to determine whether each behavior is something they are neutral about or want to encourage or discourage, and what they do to change the behavior. Their ways of responding to child behaviors which they consider changeworthy reflect differential strategies in handling, for example, dangerous behaviors, immature behaviors, cognitively oriented behaviors (e.g., "Asks you to read to him," "Asks lots of questions,") positive or negative emotional behaviors, on the part of the child. These parental strategies can be more or less appropriate in promoting child growth, in avoiding unnecessary confrontations, and in facilitating positive interactions. Changes in strategy over time may provide an index of increased awareness of more alternatives, of more positive discipline techniques, and of more use of language to convey parental wishes, of planful manipulation of the environment, of provision of behavioral models, etc.

Change measures are also available in bicultural program models. Such a measure of parent attitudes toward their participation in their child's education has shown positive changes as a function of participation in a Texas program with Spanish-speaking migrant families (Randall 1969).

Self-rating by Parents

Self-rating of parenting skills presents many pitfalls. The Home Start Summative Evaluation Report (High/Scope Educational Research Foundation and Abt Associates, Inc. 1972) highlights difficulties in such measurement of parenting skills. The report cites Smilansky's observations that using self-ratings of parenting skills is not a valid or useful procedure. Parents have tended to report changes "in the direction in which the program told the parents they were to change" (p. 16). Yet parent effectiveness ultimately must be expressed by parent behaviors and communicated understandings. In-home observations and semistructured interviews may elicit changes toward increased understanding and effectiveness without the pitfalls of self-ratings.

Parental prognosis for sustained involvement with child education. Instruments are being developed to assess parents' views about child education projects. Lally and Wright (1973) have created the Parent Evaluation of Program (PEP) for interviewing mothers whose infants have been in a child care center from 6 months to 36 months; they have also developed the PEPPER—Parent Evaluation of Program and Prognosis for Educational Responsibility—(Lally and Wright 1973) for interviewing parents whose five-year-old children are completing the open education program at the Syracuse University Children's Center. A copy of the PEPPER form is found in the Appendix.

Below are some typical responses of mothers, interviewed when their children were three years of age, to two of the questions concerning the impact of their home visitors or Child Development Trainers (CDTs).

1. If your CDT has helped you, how has she been the greatest help?

"The different exercises that she has taught."

"Trying to teach my child what she has.

52

If left to me, I couldn't have done it. I couldn't do it working nights and all."

"She kept me informed about everything."

2. *What are the qualities that make your CDT effective in working with you?*

"I feel I'm equal to her. She never puts me down. And you know that she has the same problems—just normal everyday people who don't try to run your life. She knows that everyone is different."

"She has always been friendly and helpful in any way she could. Always there to contact for any problem."

"She's very understanding. She's gone through a lot with me. I don't answer the door or phone. It takes a person with a lot of nerve to try to see me. If she weren't so patient and understanding my child wouldn't be in the center. I don't think most people would put up with someone like me. I know I wouldn't!"

"She's patient. I'm awfully moody at times."

"She's never down or mean though she has problems, too."

"She's given help on personal problems and taken us to her home. She's helped me out of certain personal jams."

"She's frank with you. She tells you what she thinks about things. You can believe her. She doesn't twist things."

"She's not afraid to come into my house and eat my cooking."

"She worked her schedule around mine."

"The way she puts things gives me choices; though she tells me when she's upset by something I've done."

"She's always there to contact for every problem."

"She likes her job more than just for the money."

"She's one of the best friends I've got."

Other measures. Further references which may be helpful in formulating a policy of evaluating childcare practices and parental achievements are: Baldwin and Baldwin 1973; Bell 1964; LaCrosse 1969; Radin and Glasser 1965; Rheingold 1960; and Roe and Siegelman 1963.

5

Why Parent Involving Is Sometimes a Hard Job

All parent involvement workers have heard sad stories from one another of failure—intermittent, steady, or initial. "Failure" may take the form of three out of twenty-five parents showing up for a group meeting where free transportation and baby-sitting are provided and topics are selected by parents. "Failure" may be the fifth rescheduled home visit when a parent still can't be found at home. "Failure" may be the lack of parental action in response to warmly extended invitations to visit the child's classrooms or nursery. "Failure" may be a home visitor's resentment rather than understanding when a parent doesn't keep appointments or enthusiastically carry out suggested activities with the child. Some of the difficulties in involving parents can be understood if we look at special problem situations and reasons for behaviors.

Parent has difficulty in seeing self as educator and responsible person in the life of the child. A home visitor needs to find ways to support a parent's awareness of primary responsibility for the health, education, and emotional development of the young child. As the responsible person in the life of the child, the parent can, however, go to outside experts for help. From this point of view, the activities and games a home visitor introduces are to assist parents in realizing their role more fully. Gordon and Lally (1967) clearly state that their learning activities are presented "as an aid to parents. We see it as a beginning from which parents can create their own games suited to their individual child" (p. 3).

Understanding between a home visitor and a parent will

grow when the visitor recognizes his or her role as *reinforcing* such creativity and responsibility on the part of the parent.

Parent Educator needs to use parents as a valued resource. The success of a parent education effort may depend on clear communication of feelings of respect, appreciation, trust, and value which program personnel extend to parents. Concrete actions are important in conveying such appreciation. One way to improve the program's care for the children and to show respect for the parent's role is to use the parent as a valued resource. *Ask a parent's advice:* "What do *you* cook and how do you fix it so that your child likes to eat it?" "How do *you* get him to laugh?" "How do *you* get her to try a new food or an activity that's somewhat difficult for her to do?" "When he's upset what kinds of things do *you* do that seem to make him feel better?"

Lack of group work skills by parent involvers. If home visitors are also expected to lead groups as well as do individual work with mothers, additional training may be needed. This may be true too if early childhood specialists in the classroom are also asked to lead parent involvement groups. In Stern's bilingual program, group meetings did not work because one mother was so domineering and talked so much that the other mothers wouldn't come to meetings. Group leaders must be sensitive to orchestrate for self-confidence as well as a fair turn in group meetings for each participant. The qualification of being able to speak Spanish, an Indian language, or another language fluently may need to be added to the professional skills required of parent involvement personnel.

Caution: Sometimes group leaders mistake parents' sociability and enjoyment in group meetings for growth in parents toward becoming educational change agents.

Parent fears. Example: A young unwed mother recently arrived in a city from a rural background may be terrified of institutions or "power-structure" people as she views teachers or social workers or home visitors. Successful parent involvement may necessitate long-time home visitation by a paraprofessional with whom the young mother can identify and feel comfortable, and with whom she gradually develops a trusting relationship. Day care center visits or workshop participation may not occur for a long while with this mother. Before venturing into the school for a visit, she may become willing to share her own home with a few other mothers to discuss a topic of interest. Later she may be asked to join a few other mothers in another home. Gradually her sphere of comfort may broaden to include visits to and more active participation within the school setting.

Too many parent involvers? Some programs have a sepa-

56

rate person to handle the learning games parents need to know, another person, such as a social worker, to handle personal problems and concerns, and a nutrition-health specialist to handle problems in those areas. In her program, discussed earlier, Earladeen Badger sometimes refocused the comments of her workshop mothers back on their cognitive interactions with children by reminding the mothers of the psychiatrist or psychologist whom they also were scheduled to see during the week and with whom they could talk about behavior problems and discipline. By contrast, at Lally's Children's Center, the home visitor deals with an ever-widening range of problems and topics of interest to the parents: education, sex, legal problems, nutrition, housing, health care, job training, etc. If too many agency people come into a home, a parent may "con" them or tune out closeness with *any* of them. Projects may need to examine whether their model works more effectively with a single or a pair of parent involvers.

The parent has too many personal problems. When there are too many economic and personal-social stresses upon a caregiving adult, child care interactions may become poor—more infrequent, more punitive, or more indifferent. Perhaps grandma is nagging and overburdening a young teenage mother. Perhaps a mother's boy friend has left her for someone else and she feels abandoned. Perhaps this infant has a more irritable temperament or needs feeding and attention more frequently than a previous child. Perhaps food stamps were stolen from the parent recently.

The home visitor needs in all cases to provide understanding and support for a parent under much stress. The visitor needs much patience and respect for the different ways and time schedules by which adults come to new competencies in the ability to handle personal crises. Most important is to win trust, acceptance, and respect. If the visitor is a friend, a listener, and a practical helper for the family with knowledge about where to go for legal aid, health care, planned parenthood assistance, housing help, then she or he may also be accepted as a source of ideas specifically to do with facilitating and optimizing children's development.

Perhaps parent visitors need to role-play more during their training sessions. Role-playing in which parent involvers take turns playing the parent and the home visitor, for example, may help home visitors become more nonjudgmental and feel more empathy for the troubles and fears which may detract from a parent's ability to do or act with the child as the home visitor would prefer.

Good examples of acceptance are to be seen in Badger's videotapes referred to in an earlier section. Some mothers seemed to sleep through some of the group meetings. Others showed varying degrees of ability or willingness to participate in the group. All mothers were accepted. All new entrants to the parent's group were made warmly welcome.

Strategies for setting up an effective model need to be developed. If crises are frequent in the lives of project families, a Crisis Center may be set up on a 24-hour telephone basis. Project staff and possibly psychiatric interns at nearby hospitals may be recruited to be available through this service for on-phone reassurance, counseling, and referrals. In some Head Start programs, psychiatric social workers on the social service staff provide such services, as well as crisis-prevention services.

Sometimes special situations may be arranged which help promote rapid development of trust. A "retreat" house in the countryside to which a dozen or more families and some project staff can be invited for a weekend of playing, discussing, cooking, eating, learning together, and getting to know one another has been used by several projects.

Programmed workshops for building, creating, cooking, repairing, discussing problems together may not only boost skills and pride in accomplishment but promote that trust between the project staff and parent which is so necessary for growth experiences to occur.

Patience is necessary because parents change gradually. The parent educator, aside from his or her work skills, needs a great store of faith and patience. This patience may need to extend for weeks or months or years of regular contacts with a family during which alternatives to and expansions of present behaviors are suggested, modeled, explained, and supported. A parent may continue to spank, for example, but has now learned to offer reasons along with the whack on the backside. The parent may be gradually learning to look for storm signals of trouble and arrange things ahead of time so as to avoid pitched battles. A parent may now try expressing understanding of a child's wishes and feelings, though the parent may continue to do things as he or she prefers. Such parent communications can alleviate a child's resentments (Ginott 1965).

That such changes in the feelings and beliefs of parents can gradually take place is vividly reflected in statements of mothers from the 33 Parent and Child Centers which serve urban and rural poverty areas across the United States (Johnson 1972-73).

> PCC made me a mother—before that I just gave birth—I used to run around with men a lot and I felt the kids just bogged me down—but now I really enjoy them.

58

Made me feel a lot more comfortable about being a mother—I used to whip the children—but I don't do that any more.

With children I used to lose my patience. They taught me how a child of certain ages should act so I gradually became a better mother. I was able to control my temper and respond in a better attitude. I didn't know how to handle their fighting and screaming. Then I saw how PCC teachers operated and I learned.

I've learned that kids are individuals—before I just raised them—clothed and fed them. Now I'm aware of even little differences and praise them and give them credit for what they can do at their own speed. I feel therefore I'm a better parent, and an important person. Before I felt that anyone could do this job.

I used to whip first and ask questions later.

I love the children a lot more. There are things that you don't appreciate until you learn about them. You appreciate them for what they are, little individuals. You can't love a child enough. Before I didn't really like children.

I feel more adequate as a person, my life has meaning to it. My relationship to my husband has improved because I have been able to stand up to him in showing him how important a woman's role is.

I'm the best example. Three years ago I didn't talk to anybody. Now I'm on the school board, and the welfare board, and I speak to anybody. (pp. 1-2)

The parent doesn't believe anyone has no ulterior motive. Such parents may often test the home visitor, break appointments, or not answer a knock at the door. They don't believe someone can value them or their ideas. Trust is built slowly. The home visitor needs to assure the parents by persistence in coming back, and by actions—such as not running in and rushing through the home visit—which show the parents they are cared about. *The parent involver should very much want to know parents' goals for their children and to help parents more effectively achieve these goals.* The home visitor is both a parent and a child advocate and must express this interest in the parent. The home educator wants to be supportive of, rather than a substitute for, parents. But a parent may need to test the home visitor's sincerity. "Dos and Don'ts of Parent Education" have been suggested by Gordon (1972a) to help build this trust.

1. When parent and child are interacting, or parent is trying to get the child to attend, don't interrupt.

2. Keep your explanations short. Break it up in steps or pieces and intersperse throughout.

3. Turn loose of the child's attention as soon as you can.

4. Summarize and review at the end of the activity using parent-child activities to discuss Desirable Parenting Behaviors.

5. Explain the WHY and the HOW of the activity.

6. Direct your attention to the parent.

7. Let the mother attend to the child's needs, unless she asks you.

8. Do not phrase a question that elicits a "NO" answer if you are not willing to accept it.

9. If you have been working on a Desirable Parenting Behavior and the parent starts using it, let her know you have observed it and how it worked.

10. Use praise and encouragement cautiously, not mechanically or in ways it will interrupt the flow of parent-child interaction.

11. Stress that the parent is the important teacher.

12. Don't offend by over or under dressing.

13. After you have explained or demonstrated, turn it loose—let the parent take over.

14. Laugh *with* and *not* at the child.

15. Don't mock the parent's language—speak naturally.

16. Don't be afraid to admit when you have made a mistake.

To Gordon's "Dos and Don'ts" we should like to add that *people learn to give if they are given to.* Home education staff may decide to give parents gifts; a stage-appropriate toy for baby; a United States Department of Agriculture pamphlet on sewing or making play equipment; a trip to the zoo in staff cars for parents and children; pictures of the children in activities and interactions in the child care center.

The parent learns what *but not* how *with the child.* Parents may have learned to sit and label pictures in a picture book, for example, and use clear verbalizations and pointing. But they may be less sensitive to the speed with which they move from picture to picture in comparison to their preschooler's readiness to take in a new picture or to repeat a new verbal label after the parent. Again, just as the process of home visitation may be critical in presenting a model of caring, practical helpfulness and readiness to move more or less quickly into new activities depending on the family's readiness, so the *process of parental involvement with children's learning activities is often more crucial than the exact content of a home curriculum.* Emotional and cognitive development are deeply integrated in the young child, and both must be considered in any educational effort.

Home visitors need to be alert to their own tendencies to teach a game instead of a person!

If a home visitor comes clutching his or her activity sheet for the week and teaches a parent how to play a cognitive or language game by rote, then the parent, too, will be apt to rely on a task formula. The power of demonstrated enjoyment and flexibility in interacting with a young child in a teaching-learning situation may affect the parent's style more than many preachments about making the game pleasurable. The more flexibility a visitor shows in adapting task complexity and verbalization level to a child's ability, in using materials attractive to that child, and in tailoring amount of time spent to the child's attention span, the more he or she is providing models which the parent can use too in working with the child.

The home visitor conveys strong feelings that he or she, as a teacher of the child, can do a better job. Such an attitude is often pervasive in day care centers where teachers, despite official welcome signs on the door, really don't trust or encourage parent visits to classrooms. If a home visitor feels that he or she is more competent than the parent and works more with the child instead of the parent on home visits, the message will be clear. At times, it may indeed seem easier to work with a young child rather than the parent. The child cooperates in learning activities and the parent may not as yet either accept or be comfortable in the role of primary educator of her child. In fact, the visitor may very well initially be more observant of some dimensions of the child's development and more knowledgeable about appropriate and enriching activities. It is still more important that parents see that although a visitor will demonstrate an activity for them with a child, *the primary task of the visits is to help the parents learn how to interact in experiences with their own children to enrich the children's lives with increased competency and joy in accomplishment.*

Parent reports that too many children present are making home lessons chaotic. Forrester et al. (1971) have pointed out successful ways in which they enlisted sibling participation in activities as well as carried out activities with focus on a target child. The home visitor needs to model. Perhaps parents can't handle games with one child if there are three of theirs and two of their parents' children "butting in." The parent educator shows how to handle more than one child. Yet, modeling or telling may still not be enough! *A Parent Involver needs to be a Parent Reinforcer.*

In some cases, families with many children may necessitate a visit by two home education staff people at the same time. In some urban neighborhoods, where crime rates are higher, female home visitors have verbalized to the author that working in pairs makes them feel more comfortable and allows greater concentration with the target child and parent while the partner carries out activities with the other children.

Importance of attitude of parent as teacher and curriculum creator. The parent involver can increase the confidence and competence of a parent as teacher of the child through reinforcing the parent's role as teacher in a variety of ways. Some simple examples are:

> "Donna really loves to do pat-a-cake when *you* do it with her!"
>
> "Did you notice how *long* she kept trying the new game when she knew you were right by her."
>
> "That was such a good idea to get Lenny to spell easy words with colored toothpick letters. Then he can have as many letters as he needs."
>
> "I noticed when you were busy talking to me you asked Joey (2nd grade) to show pictures to Annie (four years old) and you told him he did a real good job reading to her. That was such a good idea on your part, and Joey really felt proud when you complimented him."

Parent involvers model for parents how to teach a young child; they model expectations of and appreciation for small changes in a young child's abilities. For a parent, too, they must show sincere appreciation of small and large steps forward toward positive involvement with a child's educational and social development.

Meeting dependency needs of troubled parents seems to conflict with program striving to increase parent autonomy and confi-

62

dence. Specialists stress how responsible parents are for their children's development. Yet a young mother may have become pregnant without wanting this child. She may feel inadequate at mothering and at home management skills. She may feel strong dependency needs of her own. One approach may be to emphasize "what's in it for mama." More emphasis can be given to the joys and pride parents can take in noticing small developmental advances, cute sayings, new coping behaviors. The parent may need more understanding of the advantages of early attentive and responsive parenting in preventing troubles in school and in getting along with others later on.

The movement from dependency to autonomy is a slow process during a child's early years. Erikson (1963) and Sears (Sears, Maccoby, and Levin 1957) have taught us that for young children, autonomy, initiative, and independence are built upon earlier trusting and dependent relationships with nurturant caregivers. So also with some parents, building skillful initiatives in parenting, teaching, self-actualization, and in managing a household and problems of living may require that the parent educator provide dependable support and meet a great many needs of the parent.

Particularly, a young parent or a parent overwhelmed by multiple problems may have to have some of his or her "needs for know-how" met by a caring person until the parent comes, through practice and the friendship experience, to increase

> in self-assurance,
>
> in responsibility for parenting,
>
> in competent learning-facilitation interactions with the young child, and
>
> in knowledge of how to use community resources and agencies.

The problem of "weaning" a parent from the parent educator will be eased if the ultimate goals of independent functioning are strongly held and actively encouraged by the persons working with families. The timetable for achieving such functioning may, however, vary widely for each family. Case conferences which explore each situation based on the functioning of each individual family will help alert staff to the ultimate goal of tuning parents into their preeminent role in the child's early learning career in addition to the nurturance of physical and social development.

What seems like an overly dependent relationship between a parent and a parent educator may more likely represent the modeling of skills and "how to" behaviors by the helping person. Escorting a parent to a health facility, showing a parent how to market and to budget money economically—these represent ways of teaching parents how to cope with important daily problems. They can result in more, not less, independent functioning.

Other helpful and supportive friendly acts by a parent educator serve to build trust, communication, and feelings of being cared about. These acts, too, will facilitate self-assurance and feelings of self-worth so intrinsic to independent functioning.

Parent involving is brief and haphazard because staff is involved in all-day group care of children. When parent involvement is primarily carried out by teachers within the school at contact times such as going home for the day, attitudes of acceptance toward parents are even more crucial. No tired parent at 6:00 P.M. wants to be told by a teacher how impossible Joan was all day. Training of teachers whose role will include informal involvements with parents should emphasize positive ways to share information, concerns, and suggestions so that parents feel they and the teacher share, without accusations on either side, the adult responsibilities of helping children cope better with living and learning situations.

A parent may feel left out of what is going on in the child's preschool or day care center. Classroom teachers can do a great deal to bridge the gap between school and home by making home visits, getting acquainted with families, and learning more about children to help individualize teacher responsiveness and program for each child. In Project Change, a project which emphasizes open classroom education, teachers

> set out to establish a successful parent involvement program in our classroom . . . through making home visits of the children in our class. . . . The things we learned really could fill a book. Some examples are: (1) a child with rather severe small muscle coordination problems comes from an ultra immaculate home where we are sure no "messy" work is ever done and is an only child of a very protective mother, (2) a very stubborn, attention-getting little girl comes from a home where mother consistently talks about how superior the other children are to the kindergartener—meanwhile the 5-year-old is being completely obnoxious and refuses to do anything the mother says. . . .
>
> In connection with fostering positive parent-teacher relationships we held a get-acquainted-night, dish-to-pass

supper for the kindergarten child and his or her parents. The children really "sold" the idea and over 250 parents or relatives turned out (98% attendance). In preparation, we role-played the parent-child supper-sharing situation so the children would know how to show their parents around and explain different centers and areas of our room. Next year we are going to make it a point to provide transportation and personally contact the parents we feel might not come.

As additional home visit spin-off, Tuesday mornings parents come in to help with interest centers such as cooking, arts and crafts, sewing, woodworking, and science. (Puit and Totman 1974, pp. 25-27)

Whenever a child care project has separate personnel for school and for home functioning, then a home visitor needs to see one facet of his or her role as a liaison person between the child care facility and the home. A monthly newsletter may help a family feel closer to a program. "Memo to Mommy"—a brief note safety pinned to a toddler's clothing each day at the Syracuse University Children's Center before the children board their bus for home—helps teachers share a special feeling, new skills, new activities, and enjoyments of each child with each family.

The visitor needs to talk about what the children do in classrooms. What home games would reinforce or complement a given activity cycle, such as clothing or transportation or people-in-families units, which may be going on in school? Parents may give the home visitor usable junk, such as egg cartons they have saved, as their contribution for center activities. Are there photographs of the children taken to share with parents? Do the children take some of their creations home to show their folks?

Parents with increasing self-confidence and participation may want to plan social events for preschool personnel and families to get together. An Open House, a weekend retreat, a bake sale to raise money to buy special equipment for a child care center, a family paint-and-patch day at the school, are some ideas.

Need for awareness of the possibility of disparate goals and methods of parents and teacher. Prescott (1965) has gathered data on similarities and differences in values, goals, and discipline methods of parents and teachers for children in day care. Exchanging information in this manner can be illuminating for both teachers and parents and can help them understand each other's functioning better.

In general, the answers to our questions suggested that teachers were more demanding than parents in those areas of behavior that are important for maintaining order and the smooth functioning of routine. As a group, they had higher standards for neatness and table manners, were more restrictive with regard to noise, and placed more emphasis on care of property. Parents, on the other hand, had higher standards in those areas of behavior that had moral connotations. They were apt to consider it important to prevent the use of bad words; they tended to disapprove of aggression against adults. They were more likely to insist on proper sex-role behavior and to consider prevention of masturbation important.

Teachers had lower expectations for younger than for older children. Parents, however, reported few differences in expectations according to age of child. . . .

Parents of low economic status tended to be stricter than other parents on all items except neatness and table manners, self-defense, and eating. The areas of greatest difference between low- and high-income parents were those concerning noise, bad words, sexual play, aggression toward both peers and adults, and independence and self-sufficiency.

On the whole, parents of low income had higher expectations of mature behavior than did those in higher socioeconomic groups. They were less permissive of aggression, sexual play, and dependency, which may suggest that parents of high income are more likely to value initiative. This seems further indicated by the preference that low-income parents expressed for obedient children.

With regard to manners, neatness, and care of property, teachers in centers serving the higher income families had lower expectations than the parents whom they served. They were more strict, however, regarding noise and peer aggression.

Teachers in low-income centers were more permissive than those in the others. They had much lower expectations in almost all areas of behavior except modesty and "sex play." But teachers in these centers were less likely than the others to show affection for individual children. (pp. 21-22)

These data suggest that teachers often have different expectations for middle- and low-income children. Less affection and low expectations mean lower quality education for children from low-income families. The child receives an education that is not developmentally appropriate or optimal. The parent may then be forced into an adversary position with the school, if the parent insists on his or her child's right to quality education.

In contrast to these findings, a more encouraging view of the congruence of parent and teacher goals for children has been reported by Elardo and Caldwell (1973). They asked teachers, parents, and aides to check lists of possible developmental objectives for children in inner-city intervention programs. Apart from higher parental acceptance of aggression, agreement was very high between parents and staff on most goals for young children.

"Lessons" may have negative meaning for a parent; and teaching by project personnel may be on too abstract a level. Many parents have had failure experiences in schools. They may remember a teacher as someone who made them feel "put down." It may not be a pleasure at first to have a parent educator stress the "teacher" aspects of work with families. Later, parents may come to see that they can be the kind of teacher of their own children whom they themselves would have loved to have had!

Additionally, program inputs may sometimes be delivered at too abstract a level. There is occasional difficulty with "just talk and lectures" as a method of communicating new ideas and of people-changing.

Workshop experiences in making equipment and role-playing a variety of uses for materials may make a difference in helping parents see themselves as active educators. Child development films may serve as galvanizers for sharing new ideas. Mothers in Badger's program enjoyed demonstrating (for the parent group) with their own children the activities they had carried out in the home during the week. Parents may learn skills in parent education meetings and practice these activities as classroom volunteers as well as in the home. Some programs give parents who have gained competence special chances to show that competence. Gordon's Back Yard Centers hired former paraprofessional home visitors as directors. Levenstein's program successfully used as Toy Demonstrators mothers who had been recipients of the program in a former year.

Maybe we don't make the information taught to parents "jazzy" enough and fun for them so they know firsthand learning isn't a "drag" or a "terror," but can be interesting, useful, sometimes amusing, sometimes even a delight. One example is a Nutrition News item for parents in the Kentucky Rural Child Care Project's *Newsletter* (1972).

That Great American Institution—the hot dog—has recently become the target of criticism by nutritionist and consumer advocates. They claim that the 15 billion "franks" we now consume every year may contain ingredients one wouldn't want to discover on a pet food label.

In the last 25 years, the hot dog has gone from 19% fat and 19.6% protein to 28% fat. Only 11.7% now is protein and such protein! Animal ears, snouts, esophagi and lips, unidentified chicken parts and, in some cases, a sprinkling of rodent hair and insect fragments have found their way into the casing. The other ingredients are water, chemical additives (sodium nitrate, sodium acid pyrophosphate, etc.), salt, spices and "extenders" such as cereals, vegetable flour and dried milk.

It has been observed that without the chemicals "the hot dog would lose its pink blush and turn the color of unwashed sneakers." Frankfurters are a slightly better food buy than sneakers, but only slightly; if based on protein content, their price, ounce for ounce, would amount to approximately $10 per pound. And for that, as any housewife knows, you could buy at least 8 pounds of hamburger. (p. 7)

Parent involvers become discouraged. Lally (1969b) has elucidated beautifully many of the difficulties which occur over time in implementation of a home visit program. For example, one of the difficulties he discusses is:

Missionary zeal which later turned to disillusionment or boredom with day-to-day functioning.

Motivation during the initial training phase was very high. The Parent Educators saw themselves in a new and exciting role which had social consequence. The staff became aware very early of the fact that the Parent Educators were seeing the changes they would bring about as tremendously significant and almost immediate. Discussion groups were conducted which dealt with the reality of long-range rather than short-range changes in the behavior of children but these were mostly ignored. Once the Parent Educator began her field work this enthusiasm lagged. She came in contact with resistant mothers, data collection chores and children whose ability varied despite her energetic training. . . . Many Parent Educators blamed themselves or the materials for this lack of rapid intellectual growth. (p. 24)

Lally reports that individual case conferences were scheduled to help parent educators work through such feelings.

If discouragement with a given family leads a parent educator to concentrate on working with the young child rather than to continue efforts to involve the parent in educational activities with the child, case conferences and careful refocusing on the goals of the parent involvement program may need to be carried out.

Lack of supportive supervision for parent involvers. The job of a home visitor can be at times a lonely and frustrating one. A home visitor needs a supervisor who can reassure, offer suggestions, remind him or her of techniques used more successfully with other families, serve as a sounding board for complaints, as a morale-booster for flagging faith that patience and real friendliness and interest in the family's development will win out over mistrust or apathy (Wright 1973). Experts from several fields may be brought in as resource persons by the supervisor to help with specialized information in nutrition, behavior management, etc. Wright, who served for several years as supervisor of the home visitors for the Syracuse University Family Development Research Program, has noted that *flexibility* is the key word to describe the home visiting program. Hours of visitation were changed to suit parent work schedules. The supervisor had to be prepared, particularly at the outset, for daily phone calls from home visitors with problems to discuss. The supervisor didn't expect immediate expertise in all areas from the home visitors. She did ensure that weekly record keeping was up-to-date and that she held weekly case conferences for exchange of ideas on handling various problems. She allowed the home visitors a good deal of time to gain rapport and confidence of a family before she went along on a supervisory home visit as a nonparticipant observer. A corollary of provision of supportive supervision is the opportunity for parent involvement personnel to offer suggestions and ideas which they believe will expand their knowledge and skills. Parent Educators should be active contributors to their own in-service training agenda. These contributions in conjunction with sensitivity to the needs and situations of the families served will tend to increase the relevance of staff training programs.

Lack of awareness of subtle program detractions. For example: the project secretary's telephone voice—is it welcoming? Are assurances of interest and appreciation given to the caller? Are messages taken and feedback occurring?

How do bus drivers and bus riders who pick up and deliver the children behave toward families? Do they handle children with gentleness and affection as they help with transfers to and from the bus? Do they greet parents—even not-on-time parents—with courtesy?

Do program personnel consult with parents to determine the times most convenient and appropriate for holding meetings and workshops? Do program personnel promise parents written feedback on child assessments or copies of photographs of their children and then follow through as promptly as is possible on the promises? Do program personnel offer parents full explanations of assessment procedures used?

Is the center location as close to the neighborhoods served as is practicable?

Are culturally and ethnically familiar and preferred foods served frequently to the children? Are parents invited to come to lunch with the children?

These and other procedural, location, and personnel questions need to be answered in the affirmative if meaningful communication of positive intentions of the program toward the community served is to take place.

6

Additional Resources for Parents and Parent Involvers

Many projects which are actively committed to promoting parent involvement in their children's educational and social development have created manuals for parents, informational materials, or position papers which can be helpful to those who wish to carry through a parent involvement program from conceptualization of model, through process and content of implementation, to evaluation. Many of these materials have been referenced earlier as particular programs and issues have been discussed.

Bibliographies. Parent materials specifically for infant education are additionally referenced through ERIC by Honig (1973). The Educational Resources Information Center (ERIC) Clearinghouse on Early Childhood Education also has available two other biliographies which focus on mother-child home learning programs and on parent education programs (Brown 1972; Howard 1972). Some home-based child development program resources have been referenced by O'Keefe (1973a). Chilman (1974) has surveyed the research findings from programs for low-income parents.

Activities for parents and children. The Cooperative Extension Home Economics Division (1970) in New York State has published a series of materials for parents of preschoolers which focus on managing behaviors such as stuttering and stealing, dealing with issues of prejudice and sex education, and creating art activities with cast-off materials in the home. Golick (1969) discusses for parents the special problems of children with learning disabilities.

Other states have educational materials and ideas available to parents for help with socialization and education of young children. The Cooperative Extension Service, Auburn University, Auburn,

Alabama, for example, has published four-page leaflets for parents. Some titles are, "Let's Make Cloth Picture Books," and "Let's Make Puzzles." The Cooperative Extension Service, Columbia, Missouri, has put out an illustrated booklet for parents entitled "Isn't It Wonderful How Babies Learn" (Blossom 1970). "Odds and Ends: Learning Activities for Preschoolers" is an Extension Bulletin available from the University of Delaware (French n.d.).

From the Division of Home Economics, Federal Extension Service of the United States Department of Agriculture (1966), inexpensive brochures designed to be brief, informative, easy-to-read, and attractive guides for parent participation in child education are available. Titles include: "Talk With Baby;" "Fun With Circles;" "Learning Different Shapes;" "Babies Look and Learn;" and "Helping Parents Teach Young Children."

Haiman (1972) has created a series of brief, illustrated pamphlets particularly written for low-income minority group parents. Pamphlets available are: "Soul Mother;" "Kids Copy Their Parents;" "Keep Babies Busy;" and "When Kids Fight Over Toys."

Audiovisual resources. Audiovisual materials are also available to parent involvement programs. High/Scope Educational Research Foundation (1973) has produced videotape instructional programs—"Parental Support of Early Learning and Home Visitor Training"—which are for rental. Also commercially available are filmstrips on preparing for parenthood, information on the infancy period, and understanding early childhood and learning (Parents' Magazine 1973a, 1973b). Media Projects, Inc. (1971), has created a series of pamphlets plus records which provide a variety of games and ideas to help parents encourage their infants' and preschoolers' learning careers. CRM Productions has films for rental on language development and infancy which would be useful for parent group training.

From Modern Talking Picture Service, films which can be useful in training are available, without charge to educational programs. Some of the Vassar College Series films, particularly "Learning to Learn in Infancy," produced by L. Joseph Stone, would be fine choices when audiovisual materials are needed for work with prenatal parent education groups or with parents of infants. Caldwell's film "How Babies Learn," and the Head Start film "Jenny is a Good Thing," are other films also available without charge which would provide fine focal points for discussion groups on parent involvement with early learning. From the Houston, Texas, Parent-Child Development Center, the film "Parents and Children: The Gold of the Barrio," which documents their program with Mexican-American families, is available for one-week periods.

72

There are of course extensive audiovisual and written materials available in the literature on early child care programs which can provide bases for good discussions, demonstrations, and information sharing for parent involvement program personnel. One such reference, *Ideas That Work with Young Children* (Adams and Garlick 1979) covers a wide range of creative activities and approaches with young children in the classroom.

Additional available materials for parent activities with young children are: Badger 1977; Baratta-Lorton 1975; Beck 1975; Belton and Terbough 1974; Braga and Braga 1976; Caldwell 1971; Cole et al. 1972; Cole et al. 1976; Coley 1973; Conner 1976; DeLange 1976; Hannibals 1978; Jenkins and MacDonald 1979; Johnson and Johnson 1976; Kamii and Lee-Katz 1979; Karnes 1978; Marzallo and Lloyd 1974; Morreau 1972; Munnion and Grender 1976; Nimnicht et al. 1971; Painter 1971; Parents as Resource Project 1971; Rabinowitz et al. 1973; Rice and Flatter 1979; Stein and Lottick 1971; University of the State of New York n.d.; Wilms 1975; Wilt 1977.

Programs for parents of infants. A number of new programs have been designed specifically for infants and their parents. The following sources are valuable for information about programs, ideas, and materials that may be used in similar services to families: Badger 1977; Brazelton 1969, 1973; Caplan 1979; Coll et al. 1977; Cooper 1973; Gordon 1977; Haney 1978; Hersh and Levin 1978; Honig 1978a; Kagan 1978; Jew 1974; Lally and Gordon 1977; Lasater et al. 1975; Lehane 1976; Lief 1979; Packer et al. 1979; Pierson 1973; Segal 1974; Segal and Adcock 1976, 1979a, 1979b; Sitnick et al. n.d.; Sroufe 1978; Sroufe and Waters 1977; Stevens and Mathews 1978; White 1975; Wight and Corey 1974; Wilson 1977.

*Parents as childrearers.** Many programs are now available to help parents become more skillful on communicating with children and in rearing them effectively.

Parent Effectiveness Training (P.E.T)

Perhaps the most popular and widespread program for involving parents in groups to help them understand and deal better with their children is the Parent Effectiveness Training system developed by Thomas Gordon (1970, 1976). Several very important principles are taught to parents, who participate in a series of weekly classes. P.E.T. techniques are designed to help parents discard their

---

*This section is adapted from "Working with Parents of Preschool Children" by A.S. Honig. In *Parent Education and Intervention Handbook,* edited by R. Abidin, 1980. Courtesy of Charles C. Thomas, Publishers, Springfield, Illinois.

usually unsatisfactory ways of handling conflicts with children and develop more effective "no-lose" conflict-resolution methods. P.E.T. instructors teach parents to stop sending ineffective "you-messages" (such as "You've made a real mess of my living room!") and learn to send "I-messages" (such as "I feel real upset when my living room looks messy and I am afraid company may drop in.") when the behavior of a child interferes with the parents' lives. Gordon teaches that the most effective message to motivate children to change behavior that bothers parents is a simple sharing of how their behavior makes the parent feel and how it affects the parent's life. P.E.T. advocates "active listening" on the principle that when children encounter difficulties and want to share their troubles, they need parents to listen—not to talk or preach at them. You-messages can be sent that assure the child that his or her feelings count, that the parent really cares. For example, if Joey comes home from playing outside, kicks at the front door, and looks very grumpy, the parent participating in a P.E.T. group learns to say something like: "It sure looks like you had a tough time today. Seems as if maybe you had some troubles out there."

Systematic Training for Effective Parenting (STEP)
Materials are provided by Dinkmeyer and McKay (1976) for nine parent group sessions. Group discussion centering around playlets presented via audiotape by the group facilitator cover the following topics:

> Understanding the Goals of Children's Behavior and the Goals of Misbehavior;
> Understanding How Children Use Emotions to Involve Parents;
> Encouragement;
> Communication: Listening;
> Communication: Exploring Alternatives and Expressing Your Ideas and Feelings to Children;
> Developing Responsibility;
> Decision Making for Parents;
> The Family Meeting; and
> Developing Confidence.

STEP proponents feel that the group process helps parents provide support and encouragement for each other. The handbooks, posters, audiotapes, and charts come in a large carrying case easy to transport.

Avoiding the pitfalls of either permissive or authoritarian parenting is difficult for some parents. Baumrind's research (1971) has shown that loving yet authoritative parents, who are consistent and firm in discipline, have children who are more self-reliant, secure, and effective. The P.E.T. and STEP programs attempt to teach parents specific techniques for meeting their own needs as adults and solving their problems in more satisfactory ways with their children.

Interpersonal Cognitive Problem Solving (ICPS)

Shure and Spivack (1978) have taken a problem-solving approach to training low-income parents to teach their own children to generate solutions to interpersonal problems and to foresee consequences of their own behaviors in such a way that the children can make better adjustments. The authors describe their findings to date:

> We learned that after only three months' time, overly impulsive children in normal inner-city preschools and kindergartens displayed less impatience, overemotion, and aggression. Overly inhibited children became more socially outgoing, became better liked by their peers, and showed more awareness of others' feelings . . . . To date, the most powerful ICPS mediator in young children appears to be the ability to conceptualize multiple solutions to interpersonal problems and, secondarily, the ability to anticipate the consequences of acts. (Shure and Spivack 1978, pp. 7–8)

These findings among trained preschoolers continued to hold up in comparison to control children one year later. The authors report that in their work with mothers and their preschool children, those mothers who consistently applied problem-solving techniques when actual problems came up had children who most improved in ICPS thinking skills and subsequent behavioral adjustment. The kinds of dialogues and scripts that are taught, of course, require that parents acquire new thinking skills of their own. "Training parents to think through solutions to interpersonal problems and to anticipate the consequences of acts helps them appreciate the very thinking process they in turn learn to transmit to their children" (Shure and Spivack 1978, p. 38).

Building children's self-esteem

Washington (1977) has developed a systematic program, SUCCESS, designed to help urban parents improve their effectiveness as educators and builders of self-esteem in their children by setting and resetting clear, attainable learning goals. Sometimes a parent gets angry that a child isn't "obeying" or "trying." In reality, the adult may have given vague clues as to what the desired behavioral goal is or how to tackle a requested task. Sometimes, a parent may set a task too difficult developmentally for the child at a particular level of functioning. Clarity and specificity help a child to "zero in" on aspects of a problem he or she is expected to solve.

The SUCCESS program seems a logical social application of findings from Hess and Shipman's Chicago study of Black mothers from four different income levels in learning task interactions with their preschool children. Those mothers who were better educated and whose children successfully completed the Block Sorting and Etch-a-Sketch Designs tasks gave "Specific directions and feedback, worked to elicit the child's cooperativeness, accompanied their requests for physical response with verbal explanations, and used elaborated rather than restricted language styles" (Hess 1969, p. 4).

Additional resources

Several other resources are also available for those whose educative focus is on the parent as a skillful and positive child rearer: Bell 1976; Bessell and Kelly 1978; Bigner 1979; Boulette 1975; Brazelton 1975; Briggs 1976; Brown 1976; Buxbaum 1974; Comer and Poussaint 1975; Dodson 1977; Early Childhood Program 1976; Fraiberg 1977; Freed 1977; Harrison-Ross and Wyden 1974; Jenkins 1979; Knox 1978; McLaughlin 1976; Miller n.d.; Montemayor 1977; Patterson 1971, 1976; Peck and Granzig 1978; Rinn and Markle 1977; Salk 1972, 1974; H.W. Smith 1978; Spock 1955, 1974; Waggonseller et al. 1977.

Parents as teachers. A number of sources point up the importance of parents in the educational development of their children (Abidin 1980; Bell 1976; Channing L. Bete Co. 1978; Cahoon et al. 1978; Carew et al. 1976; Carnegie Corporation of New York 1978; Cohen 1977; Croft 1979; ERIC 1977; Flood 1977; Goldberg 1978; Goodson and Hess 1975; Head Start 1968; Heinicke 1977; Honig 1979b; Lally and Honig 1977; Laosa 1978; Levenstein 1977; LINC 1975; Madden et al. 1976; Miller and Baker 1976; Morris 1974; Morrison 1978; National Right to Read 1978; "Parent Education TV Series" 1978; Parker and Kass 1975; Recruitment Leadership and Training Institute 1975; Rice and Flatter 1979; Slaughter 1979; R.A. Smith 1977; Stein 1976; Stevens 1977; Sumpter and Metger 1977; HEW 1974; Wallat and Goldman n.d.; White 1977, 1979; and Woodard 1977).

Parent-teacher references. Many publications are available to help improve parent-teacher communications, relationships, and effective working together to promote a child's development (ACEI 1969; Adair and Eckstein 1969; Auerbach and Roche 1971;

Burns, Childs, and Clark 1967; Chilman and Kraft 1963; Conant 1971; Grissom 1971; Jones 1970; Karnes 1969; Medinnus 1967; Newman 1971; Project Head Start n.d.; Thompson 1965; Weaver 1968; and Weikart 1971b).

Additional resources for training parent involvers. The Day Care and Child Development Council of America (1973) publishes an excellent guide to materials which can assist a program in training personnel as parent involvers. This listing includes such materials as a color filmstrip called "Parents and Staff Together," and publications called *Parent Programs in Child Development, Parent Involvement Staff Handbook,* and *Parents and Teachers Together: A Training Manual for Parent Involvement in Head Start Centers.* Many references on their list of publications should prove especially useful (a) to train workers in techniques of parent involvement, (b) to describe problem situations which may arise in parent involvement, such as poor family day care practices by insufficiently trained family day care personnel, and (c) to provide concrete activities, tasks, games, and recipes for parents to carry out with infants and young children.

Other sources of information and training materials include Abidin 1976; CDA 1978; Curry and Rood 1975; Fraser 1977; Gotts 1977.

There is a growing awareness of the importance of the relationship between school, home, and community in furthering the educational careers of children. Many publications are now available that can assist teachers toward more effective communication with parents in order to promote optimal child development and learning (Beebe 1976; Bennett and Henson n.d.; Coletta 1976; Croft 1979; Gallagher 1976; Kroth 1978; Nedler 1977; Nedler and McAfee 1979; Robison 1977).

Some final suggested references which can be useful for training personnel who will be involving parents in their children's early education or will be developing organizational skills and techniques for working with parent groups are: Abraham 1974; ACEI 1974; Becker 1971; Becker and Becker 1974; Beebe 1976; Bennett and Milner 1979; Berlin and Berlin n.d.; Bradley and Caldwell 1976; Champagne and Goldman 1971; Dodson 1971; Freeberg and Payne 1967; Gallagher 1976; Gordon 1969b, 1970b, 1972b, 1976; Head Start 1977, n.d.; Hess 1969; Hess et al. 1971; Hoffman 1972; Horton 1971; Jackson and Stretch 1976; Kapfer 1977; Kifer 1976; Klaus and Kennell 1976; Larrabee 1969, 1974; Lawrence 1975; Office of Child Development 1972, 1973; O'Keefe n.d., 1978; Parent-Child Development Center 1975; Pavloff and Wilson 1972; Pickarts and Fargo 1971; Piers 1955;

Powell 1978; Rich 1977; Rowen 1975; Schaefer 1977; Shoemaker 1965; Stein 1967; Weikart et al. 1971; Wilson and Wingate 1974.

Program supervisory personnel should note that some parent involvement personnel, whether paraprofessional or professional, may not come from a cultural background which gives them special knowledge of and insight into the population with whom they are working. Those parent educators may need additional training to ensure understanding of and sensitivity to the cultural mores and customs of the families to be served. For example, Chilman (1968) has provided a helpful overview of patterns of child care in poor families and the implications for service programs. Special attention may need to be paid to understanding rural and urban settings, different ethnic backgrounds, very young parents, moderate and extreme poverty conditions, bilingualism, etc., in implementing services for families (Pavenstedt 1965; Scheinfeld 1969; Scheinfeld, Bowles, Tuck, and Gold 1969).

Conclusions

1. The parent is curriculum creator and educator. Parents are responsible for the development of their children. The parent must be seen as the responsible person by program personnel.

2. Efforts to involve parents with their young child's learning and education must be varied to meet parental and child developmental needs.

For some families this may mean day care plus home visits sandwiched in during evening hours; for other families this may mean neighbors with prior training who visit and play show-and-tell with at-home parents and preschool children.

3. Patience is a virtue. Some parent involvement efforts take a lot more "give" before they "take."

4. Parent involvement personnel are an enrichment program's catalysts, the indispensable ingredient. If they care about the development of mothers, fathers, and their children and do things to show they care, and they have knowledge, skills, and techniques, then a program can work.

5. Parent involvement means not only lessons but a *way* of working with parents, children, and lessons. Flexibility is the key concept in changing and adapting task ingredients and games so that household resources, and parent/child motivational and skill levels are taken into account.

Parent involvers must meet the problem of the match between program goals and present family functioning and needs.

Teaching styles: Modeling and demonstrating skills and caring qualities may work better than teaching by talk alone.

6. Training of parent involvers is essential. Visits alone to parents are not enough to ensure change. People need skills to help other people change and grow.

7. Paraprofessionals and professionals both can be effective parent involvers; each may have particular effectiveness working with either parents or children (Gordon and Jester 1972).

8. Looking for short-term cognitive change measures may short-change a program's value.

Social development outcomes are very important. As Zigler (1970) has noted, more important than gains in intellectual level is the fact that many parents have had experiences which have alienated them from our society. He stresses the need to give parents and children experiences that will help them to actualize themselves within the social framework. "We must be just as concerned with the development of positive attitudes and motives as with the development of the intellect" (p. 408).

9. Parent involvement is not only for the poor. Parenting skills come in all sizes and shapes and degrees in *all* families. Lots of us could use more of these skills.

10. Parent involvement is not only for those with children in day care or school programs. All babies and preschoolers in or out of such programs can use that special early learning supplement that only parents can implement on a full scale, anytime any-place basis.

With parents effectively involved in their children's development and education, none of us will be afraid to answer Kruger's (1972) challenging query: "What kinds of parents will your grandchildren have?"

Appendix

Forms used for
Parent Evaluation of Program and Prognosis for
Educational Responsibility
(PEPPER)

Lally & Wright
Family Development Research Program
Syracuse University
1973

1. Please describe in your own words what you think a typical day at the Children's Center is like for your child. _____
_____

2. Describe the treatment you generally receive from staff members.
_____

3. Does your child talk about the center when he is at home? Yes ___ No ___
What does he say? _____
_____

4. Does the schedule of the center allow you time for work, school, outside activities? Please describe. _____
_____

5. Do the teachers at the center discipline your child in the same manner that you do at home? Yes ___ No ___ How do they differ?
_____

6. How do you wish they would handle your child? _____
_____

7. What have you liked best about the program for your child? ___
_____

8. What have you liked least? _____
_____

9. Has the information that you received about the actions and feelings of young children (because of _____'s participation in

81

the program) changed the way you act with your other children?
Yes ___ No ___
Describe. _____
_____

10. Has having your child in the center affected your overall family way of life in any way? Yes ___ No ___ Please describe. _____
_____
_____

11. Which of your child's actions that you see at home, would you say were caused by his participation in the program? _____
_____

    By your participation in the home visit program?_____
_____

12. If your Child Development Trainer (CDT) has helped you, how has she been the greatest help?_____
_____

13. What are the qualities that make your CDT effective in working with you? _____
_____

14. In what ways has the Children's Center experience helped to prepare your child for school? _____
_____

15. What do you think your job will be in educating your child once he gets into school?_____
_____

16. Has the Children's Center experience helped you prepare yourself for this job? Yes ___ No ___
In what way? _____
_____

17. What do you think will happen to your child in school? _____
_____

18. How much influence can parents have on the school system? __
_____

19. Name everything that you can think of that will make it possible for your child to succeed in school. _____
_____

References

Abidin, R. R., ed. *Parent Education Handbook.* Springfield, Ill.: Charles C. Thomas, 1980.

Abidin, R. R. *Parenting Skills: Trainer's Manual and Workbook.* New York: Human Sciences Press, 1976.

Abraham, W. *Parent Talk* (a set of 12 monthly articles for parents of preschoolers). Scottsdale, Ariz.: Sunshine Press, 1974–1979.

Adair, T., and Eckstein, E. *Parents and the Day Care Center.* New York: Federation of Protestant Welfare Agencies, 1969.

Adams, L. D., and Garlick, B., eds. *Ideas That Work with Young Children, Volume 2.* Washington, D.C.: National Association for the Education of Young Children, 1979.

Adkins, D. C. *Final Report on Programmatic Research on Preschool Language, Quantitative, and Motivation Curricula Combined with Parent Participation—1969–70.* Honolulu, Hawaii: University of Hawaii Center for Research in Early Childhood Education, 1971a.

Adkins, D. C. *Home Activities for Preschool Children: A Manual of Games and Activities for Use by Parents with Their Children at Home, to Foster Certain Preschool Goals.* Honolulu, Hawaii: University of Hawaii Center for Research in Early Childhood Education, September 1971b.

Alford, R. D., ed. *Home-Oriented Preschool Education: Curriculum Planning Guide.* Charleston, W. Va.: Appalachia Educational Laboratory, 1972.

Armstrong, B.; Boyd, J.; Mainwold, L.; and Marshall, H. *Resource Guide for Parents of Preschool Visually-Impaired Children.* Columbus, Ohio: Ohio Resource Center for the Visually Handicapped, 1978.

Association for Childhood Education International. *Communication: Parents, Children, Teachers.* Washington, D.C.: Association for Childhood Education International, 1969.

Association for Childhood Education International. *Parenting.* Washington, D.C.: Association for Childhood Education International, 1974.

Auerbach, A. B., and Roche, S. *Creating Pre-school Settings: Parental Development in an Integrated Neighborhood Project.* New York: John Wiley & Sons, 1971.

Badger, E. D. *Curriculum: Postnatal Classes for High Risk Mother-Infant Pairs.* Cincinnati, Ohio: Department of Pediatrics, University of Cincinnati College of Medicine, 1977.

Badger, E. D. "A Mother's Training Program: A Sequel Article." *Children Today* 1, no. 3 (1972): 7–11.

Baldwin, A. S., and Baldwin, C. P. "The Study of Mother-Child Interaction." *American Scientist* 61, no. 6 (1973): 714–721.

Baratta-Lorton, M. *Workjobs—for Parents.* Reading, Mass.: Addison-Wesley Publishing Co., 1975.

Barbrack, C. R., and Horton, D. M. *Educational Intervention in the Home and Paraprofessional Career Development: A First Generation Mother Study.* Nashville, Tenn.: DARCEE Papers and Reports 4 (Whole No. 1) 1970a.

Barbrack, C. R., and Horton, D. M. *Educational Intervention in the Home and Paraprofessional Career Development: A Second Generation Mother Study with an Emphasis on Costs and Benefits.* Nashville, Tenn.: DARCEE Papers and Reports 4 (Whole No. 4) 1970b.

Bartz, K. W., and Witcher, W. C. "When Father Gets Custody." *Children Today* 7 (1978): 2–6.

Bassin, J., and Drovetta, D. "Parent Outreach." *The Exceptional Parent* 6 (1976): 6–9.

Baumrind, D. "Child Care Practices Anteceding Three Patterns of Preschool Behavior." *Genetic Psychology Monographs* 75 (1967): 43–88.

Baumrind, D. "Current Patterns of Parental Authority." *Developmental Psychology* 4 (1971): 1–101.

Bayley, N., and Schaefer, E. S. "Relationships between Socio-economic Variables and the Behavior of Mothers toward Young Children." *Journal of Genetic Psychology* 96 (1960): 61–77.

Beck, J. *How to Raise a Brighter Child: The*

Case for Early Learning. New York: Pocket Books, 1975.

Beck, R. *It's Time to Stand Up for Your Children: A Parent's Guide to Child Advocacy.* Washington, D.C.: Children's Defense Fund, 1979.

Becker, W. C. *Parents Are Teachers: A Child Management Program.* Champaign, Ill.: Research Press Company, 1971.

Becker, W. C., and Becker, J. W. *Successful Parenthood.* Champaign, Ill.: Research Press Company, 1974.

Beckwith, L. "Relationships between Infants' Social Behavior and Their Mothers' Behavior." *Child Development* 43 (1972): 397–411.

Bee, H.; Van Egeren, L. F.; Pytkowicz, A. R.; Nyman, B. A.; and Leckie, M. S. "Social Class Differences in Maternal Teaching Strategies and Speech Patterns." *Developmental Psychology* 41, no. 2 (1969): 291–311.

Beebe, M. K. "Teachers and Parents Together." *Today's Education* 65, no. 3 (Sept./Oct. 1976): 74–79.

Bell, R. Q. "Structuring Parent-Child Interaction Situation for Direct Observation." *Child Development* 35 (1964): 1009–20.

Bell, T. H. *Active Parent Concern: A New Home Guide to Help Your Child Do Better in School.* Englewood Cliffs, N.J.: Prentice-Hall, 1976.

Bell, T. H. *An Educator Looks at Parenting.* Urbana, Ill.: ERIC Clearinghouse on Early Childhood Education, 1976. ED 127–547.

Bell, T. H., and Thorum, A. R. *Your Child's Intellect: A Guide to Home Based Preschool Education.* Salt Lake City, Utah: Olympus Publishing Co., 1972.

Beller, E. K. "The Evaluation of Effects of Early Educational Intervention on Intellectual and Social Development of Lower-Class, Disadvantaged Children." In *Critical Issues in Research Related to Disadvantaged Children,* edited by E. Grotberg. Princeton, N.J.: Educational Testing Service, 1969.

Belton, S., and Terbough, C. *Activities to Help Children Learn at Home.* New York: Human Sciences Press, 1974.

Bennett, L. M., and Henson, F. O. *Keeping in Touch with Parents: The Teacher's Best Friends.* Austin, Tex.: Learning Concepts, n.d.

Bennett, T., and Milner, S. "Child Care Center Teaches Parents Too." *Dimensions* 7, no. 2 (January 1979): 44–46.

Berlin, R., and Berlin, I. N. "Parents' Role in Education as Primary Prevention." Unpublished manuscript, University of Washington, Division of Child Psychiatry, Seattle, Wash., n.d.

Bessell, H., and Kelly, T. P. *The Parent Book: The Holistic Program for Raising the Emo-tionally Mature Child.* San Diego: Psych/Graphic Publishers, 1978.

Channing L. Bete Co. *Your Child's Potential to Learn.* Greenfield, Mass.: Channing L. Bete Co., 1978.

Beyer, E. "Sharing—A New Level in Teacher-Parent Relationships." Washington, D.C.: National Association for the Education of Young Children, 1959.

Biber, B. "Goals and Methods in a Preschool Program for Disadvantaged Children." Unpublished manuscript, Bank Street College of Education, New York, 1970.

Bigner, J. J. *Parent-Child Relations: An Introduction to Parenting.* New York: Macmillan, 1979.

Biller, H., and Meredith, D. *Father Power.* New York: David McKay Co., 1974.

Bing, F. "Effects of Childrearing Practices on Development of Differential Cognitive Abilities." *Child Development* 34, no. 3 (1963): 631–648.

Blossom, M. *Isn't It Wonderful How Babies Learn!* Columbia, Mo.: Cooperative Extension Service, University of Missouri, 1970.

Boger, R. B.; Kuipers, J.; Wilson, N.; and Andrews, M. *Parents Are Teachers Too.* East Lansing, Mich.: Institute for Family and Child Study, Michigan State University, 1974.

Boulette, T. R. *A Healthy Family (Una Familia Sans).* Santa Barbara, Calif.: Department of Mental Health, 1975.

Bowles, D. D., and Scheinfeld, D. R. *The Use of Toys in Expanding Mothers' Childrearing Attitudes and Skills Through a Home Teaching Program. Research Report, 1969* 6, no. 10. Institute for Juvenile Research, Chicago, Ill.

Bracken, M. "Lessons Learned from a Baby Care Club for Unmarried Mothers." *Children* 18 (1971): 133–137.

Bradley, R. H., and Caldwell, B. M. "The Relation of Infants' Home Environments to Mental Test Performance at 54 Months: A Follow-up Study." *Child Development* 47 (1976): 1172–1174.

Braga, J., and Braga, L. *Children and Adults: Activities for Growing Together.* Englewood Cliffs, N.J.: Prentice-Hall, 1976.

Brazelton, T. B. *Infants and Mothers: Differences in Development.* New York: Delta, Delacorte Press, 1969.

Brazelton, T. B. *Toddlers and Parents: A Declaration of Independence.* New York: Delacorte Press, 1975.

Brazelton, T. B. "Working with the Family." In *The Infants We Care For,* ed. L. L. Dittmann. Washington, D.C.: National Association for the Education of Young Children, 1973.

Bridgman, J.; Goodroe, P.; Horton, D.; Scanlan, J.; and Strain, B. *A Handbook for Family Day-Care Workers.* Nashville, Tenn.: Demonstration and Research Center for Early Education, George Peabody College for Teachers, 1971.

Briggs, D. C. *Your Child's Self-Esteem.* Garden City, N.Y.: Doubleday Co., 1976.

Brodsky, I. M. *The World's Newest Profession.* Philadelphia: Profession of Parenting Institute, n.d.

Bromwich, R. M. "Focus on Maternal Behavior in Infant Intervention." *American Journal of Orthopsychiatry* 46, no. 3 (1976): 439–446.

Bromwich, R. M.; Khokha, E.; Fust, L. S.; Baxter, E.; and Burge, D. *Manual for the Parent Behavior Progression (PBP).* Los Angeles, Calif.: University of California Mental Retardation Research Center, 1978.

Bronfenbrenner, U. "Developmental Research, Public Policy, and the Ecology of Childhood." *Child Development* 45 (1974): 1–5.

Bronfenbrenner, U. "Is Early Intervention Effective?" In *The Family as Educator,* ed. H. J. Leichter. New York: Teachers College Press, 1975.

Bronfenbrenner, U. *Is Early Intervention Effective. A Report on Longitudinal Evaluations of Preschool Programs.* Volume II. Washington, D.C.: Office of Child Development, United States Department of Health, Education, and Welfare, 1974.

Brophy, J. E. "Mothers as Teachers of Their Own Preschool Children: The Influence of Socioeconomic Status and Task Structure on Teaching Specificity." *Child Development* 41, no. 1 (1970): 79–94.

Brown, C. C. "It Changed My Life: A Report on Four Parent Training Programs." *Psychology Today* 10, no. 6 (November 1976): 47–57.

Brown, D. *Parent Education: An Abstract Bibliography.* Urbana, Ill.: ERIC Clearinghouse on Early Childhood Education, No. 1300–34, 1972.

Burns, D. *United Services for Effective Parenting Directory, State of Ohio.* Cincinnati, Ohio: Department of Pediatrics, University of Cincinnati College of Medicine, 1978.

Burns, L.; Childs, L.; and Clark, E. "Parents Have Much to Give." *Young Children* 23, no. 2 (1967): 110–114.

Bushell, D., Jr., and Jacobson, J. M. "The Simultaneous Rehabilitation of Mothers and Their Children." Paper presented at a meeting of the American Psychological Association, San Francisco, Calif., August 1968.

Buxbaum, E. *Your Child Makes Sense: A Guidebook for Parents.* New York: International Universities Press, 1974.

Cadman, L. A.; Fullerton, H. M.; and Wylie, E. J. *Parents Handbook: A Handbook for Parents of Preschool Handicapped Children.* Wichita Falls, Tex.: Region IX Education Service Center, 1976.

Cahoon, O. W.; Price, A. H.; and Scoresby, A. L. *Parents and the Achieving Child.* Provo, Utah: Brigham Young University, 1978.

Caldwell, B. M. *Home Teaching Activities.* Little Rock, Ark.: Center for Early Development and Education, 1971.

Caldwell, B. M. "Parent Enablement—Best Way to Meet Children's Needs." Paper presented at the Parent Education and Involvement Conference, June 1979, University of North Carolina, Chapel Hill.

Caldwell, B. M. *Preschool Inventory.* Princeton, N.J.: Educational Testing Service, 1970.

Caldwell, B. M. "What Is the Optimal Learning Environment for the Young Child?" *American Journal of Orthopsychiatry* 37, no. 1 (1967): 8–21.

Caldwell, B. M., and Honig, A. S. "The Implicit Learning Theory (IPLET) Interview." Unpublished manuscript, Syracuse University, 1965.

Caldwell, B. M., and Richmond, J. B. "Social Class Level and the Stimulation Potential of the Home." In *Exceptional Children: The Normal Infant,* edited by J. Hellmuth. Vol. 1. New York: Brunner/Mazel, 1967.

Callahan, S. C. *Parenting: Principles and Politics of Parenthood.* New York: Doubleday Co., 1973.

Cansler, D. P.; Martin, G. H.; and Valand, M. C. *Working with Families: A Manual for Early Childhood Programs Serving the Handicapped.* Winston-Salem, N.C.: Kaplan Press, 1976.

Caplan, F., ed. *Parents' Yellow Pages.* New York: Anchor Press/Doubleday, 1979.

Carew, J. V.; Chan, I.; and Halfar, C. *Observing Intelligence in Young Children.* Englewood Cliffs, N.J.: Prentice-Hall, 1976.

Carnegie Corporation of New York. "Para un Nuevo Dia en la Educación: The Chicano Education Project." *Carnegie Quarterly* 26, no. 4 (Fall 1978).

Child Development Associate Consortium. "Parents Ask . . . C.D.A. Answers." Washington, D.C.: Child Development Associate Consortium, 1978.

The CDA Program: The Child Development Associate Training Guide. Washington, D.C.: Office of Child Development, United States Department of Health, Education, and Welfare, 1973. DHEW Publication No. (OCD) 73–1065.

Champagne, D. W., and Goldman, R. M. *Stimulation Activities for Training Parents and Teachers as Educational Partners. A Report and Evaluation.* Urbana, Ill.: ERIC Clearinghouse on Early Childhood Education, 1971. ERIC Document No. ED–048945.

Chilman, C. S. "Poor Families and Their Patterns of Child Care. Some Implications for Service Programs." In *Early Child Care: The New Perspectives,* edited by L. L. Dittmann. New York: Atherton Press, 1968.

Chilman, C. S. "Child Development and Social Policy." In *Review of Child Development Research,* edited by B. Caldwell and H. Ricciuti. Vol. 3. Chicago: University of Chicago Press, 1974.

Chilman, C., and Kraft, I. "Helping Low Income Parents through Parent Education Groups." *Children* 10 (1963): 127–136.

Christopherson, E. R.; Kuehn, B. S.; Grinstead, J. D.; Barnard, J. D.; Rainey, S. K.; and Kuehn, F. E. "A Family Training Program for Abuse and Neglect Families." *Journal of Pediatric Psychology* 1 (1976): 90–94.

Clarke-Stewart, A. *Child Care in the Family.* New York: Academic Press, 1977a.

Clarke-Stewart, A. "The Father's Impact on Mother and Child." Paper presented at the biennial meeting of the Society for Research in Child Development, March 1977b, New Orleans, La.

Cohen, S. E. "Caregiver-Child Interaction and Competence in Pre-Term Children." Paper presented at the biennial meeting of the Society for Research in Child Development, March 1977, New Orleans, La.

Cole, A.; Haas, C.; Heller, T.; and Weinberger, B. *Backyard Vacation-1974.* PAR Project, 464 Central, Northfield, IL 60093. 1976.

Cole, A.; Haas, C.; Bushnell, F.; and Weinberger, B. *I Saw a Purple Cow and 100 Other Recipes for Learning.* Boston, Mass.: Little, Brown and Co., 1972.

Cole, A.; Haas, C.; Heller, T.; and Weinberger, B. *More Recipes for Fun.* PAR Project, 464 Central, Northfield, IL 60093. 1976.

Cole, A.; Haas, C.; Heller, T.; and Weinberger, B. *A Pumpkin in a Pear Tree.* Boston: Little Brown and Co., 1976.

Cole, A.; Haas, C.; Heller, T.; and Weinberger, B. *Recipes for Fun.* PAR Project, 464 Central, Northfield, IL 60093. 1976.

Cole, A.; Haas, C.; Heller, T.; and Weinberger, B. *Recipes for Holiday Fun.* PAR Project, 464 Central, Northfield, IL 60093. 1976.

Cole, A.; Haas, C.; Heller, T.; and Weinberger, B. *Still More Recipes for Fun.* PAR Project, 464 Central, Northfield, IL 60093. 1976.

Coletta, A. J. *Working Together: A Guide to Parent Involvement.* Atlanta, Ga.: Humanics, 1976.

Coley, E. D., ed. *I Can Do It.* Raleigh, N.C.: Project Enlightenment, Raleigh Public Schools, 1973.

Coll, C. G., et al. "Facilitating a Positive Interaction Between Parent and Infant in the Neonatal Intensive Care Unit." Urbana, Ill.:

ERIC Clearinghouse on Early Childhood Education, 1977. ED 140–971.

Comer, J. P., and Poussaint, A. F. *Black Child Care: How to Bring Up a Healthy Black Child in America.* New York: Simon & Shuster, 1975.

Conant, M. M. "Teachers and Parents: Changing Roles and Goals." *Childhood Education* 48, no. 3 (1971): 114–118.

Conner, J. E., and Sanders, F. J. *Enjoy Your Child at Home.* Tenn.: Educational Planning and Product Development, 1976.

Cooper, G. C. *Parenting Curriculum.* Washington, D.C.: Child Welfare League of America, 1973.

Cooper, G. C. *Teachers' Guide to Child Development Section: Parenting Curriculum for School-Age Parents.* Washington, D.C.: Consortium on Early Childbearing and Childrearing, 1974. Ordering Code No. 010–0005.

Cooper, J. O. *Parenting: Strategies and Educational Methods.* Columbus, Ohio: Charles E. Merrill, 1978.

Cooperative Extension Home Economics Division. *Parents of Preschoolers.* Ithaca, N.Y.: Cornell University, 1970.

Costello, J., and Binstock, E. *Review and Summary of a National Survey of the Parent-Child Center Program.* Washington, D.C.: Office of Child Development, United States Department of Health, Education, and Welfare, 1970.

Croft, D. J. *Parents as Teachers: A Resource Book for Home, School and Community Relations.* Belmont, Calif.: Wadsworth Publishing Co., 1979.

Curry, L. J., and Rood, L. A. *Head Start Handbook for Parents.* Washington, D.C.: Gryphon House, 1975.

Curtis, J. *Working Mothers.* New York: Doubleday and Co., 1976.

Danforth, J.; Miller, D. S.; Day, A. L.; and Steiner, G. J. "Group Services for Unmarried Mothers: An Interdisciplinary Approach." *Children* 18 (1971): 59–64.

Daniel, J. H., and Hyde, J. N., Jr. "Working with High-Risk Families." *Children Today* 4, no. 6 (Nov.-Dec. 1975): 23–25.

Datta, L. E. "Parent Involvement in Early Childhood Education: A Perspective from the United States." Paper presented at the Organization for Economic Cooperation and Development, Centre for Educational Research and Innovation Conference on Early Childhood Education, Paris, France, October 1973.

Dave, R. H. "The Identification and Measurement of Environment Process Variables That Are Related to Educational Achievement." Unpublished doctoral dissertation, University of Chicago, 1963.

Day Care and Child Development Council of America. *Voice for Children* 5, no. 1. Washington, D.C.: Day Care and Child Development Council of America, 1972.

Day Care and Child Development Council of America. *Resources for Day Care.* Washington, D.C.: Day Care and Child Development Council of America, 1973.

Day Care Council of Westchester. *Day Care News: Parental Involvement.* White Plains, N.Y., Winter 1974.

DeLange, C. M., ed. *Our Worlds, Our Words: Experiences.* Nashville, Tenn.: Intersect Press, 1976.

de Lissovoy, V. "Child Care by Adolescent Parents." *Children Today* 2 (1973): 22–25.

Dilenowisco Education Cooperative: Early Childhood Development Program. Brochure, 1032 Virginia Avenue, Norton, Va., 1973.

DHEW. *The Hassles of Becoming a Teenage Parent.* Washington, D.C.: U.S. Department of Health, Education, and Welfare, 1977a. DHEW Publication No. (HSA) 78–5624.

DHEW. *One Parent Families.* Washington, D.C.: U.S. Department of Health, Education, and Welfare, 1974a. DHEW Publication No. (OHD) 74–44.

DHEW. *A Reader's Guide for Parents of Children with Mental, Physical, or Emotional Disabilities.* Washington, D.C.: U.S. Department of Health, Education, and Welfare, 1977b. DHEW Publication No. (HSA) 77–5290.

DHEW. *Report of a Joint Conference on Home Start.* Washington, D.C.: U.S. Department of Health, Education, and Welfare, 1974b. DHEW Publication No. (OHD) 74–1072.

Dinkmeyer, D., and McKay, G. D. *Systematic Training for Effective Parenting: Parent's Handbook.* Circle Pines, Minn.: American Guidance Service, 1976.

Division of Home Economics, Federal Extension Service, United States Department of Agriculture. *Guides for Parents.* Washington, D.C.: United States Department of Agriculture, 1966.

Dodson, F. *How to Discipline with Love: From Crib to College.* New York: Rawson Associates, 1977.

Dodson, F. *How to Father.* New York: Signet Books, 1974.

Dodson, F. *How to Parent.* New York: Signet Books, 1971.

Dreskin, W. "For Young Parents: The Daycare Dilemma." *The Single Parent* 21 (1978): 9–11.

Drouillard, R., and Raynor, S. *Move It! A Guide for Helping Visually Handicapped Children.* Washington, D.C.: Physical Education and Recreation for the Handicapped Information and Research Utilization Center, 1977.

Duncan, T. R., and Duncan, D. *You're Divorced But Your Children Aren't.* Englewood Cliffs, N.J.: Spectrum Books, 1979.

Early Childhood Program, Southwest Educational Development Laboratory. Series of pamphlets: "Children Learn by Watching and Helping," "Help Your Children Cope with Frustration," "Practice What You Teach," "Expect the Best from Your Children," "Read to Your Child," "Praise Your Children," and "Pay Attention to Your Children." Southwest Educational Development Laboratory, 211 E. 7th St., Austin, TX 78701. 1976.

Early Years Parent. A magazine for parents of children 2 to 9. Early Years Parent, P.O. Box 1223, Darien, CT 06820.

Eiduson, B. T. "Child Development in Emergent Family Styles." *Children Today* 7, no. 2 (Mar.-Apr. 1978): 24–31.

Eiduson, B. T. *The Dynamics of the One Child Family: Socialization Implications.* Urbana, Ill.: ERIC Clearinghouse on Early Childhood Education, n.d. ED 130–785.

Eiduson, B. T., and Alexander, J. W. "The Role of Children in Alternative Family Styles." *Journal of Social Issues* 34, no. 2 (1978).

Elardo, R., and Caldwell, B. M. "Value Imposition in Early Education: Fact or Fancy?" *Child Care Quarterly* 2, no. 1 (1973): 6–13.

Emlen, A. C., and Watson, E. L. *Matchmaking in Neighborhood Day Care.* Corvallis, Oreg.: Oregon State University, 1971.

Emmerich, W. *Structure and Development of Personal-Social Behaviors in Preschool Settings.* An ETS-Head Start longitudinal study of disadvantaged children and their first school experiences. Report under Grant Number H-8256. Princeton, N.J., November 1971.

ERIC. *A School and Home-Based Bilingual Education Model (Nursery School—Grade 3).* Urbana, Ill.: ERIC Clearinghouse on Early Childhood Education, 1977. ED 144–705.

Erikson, E. *Childhood and Society.* New York: W. W. Norton & Co., 1963.

Family Day Care Training Project. *Progress Report.* Office of Career Development, University of Minnesota, Minneapolis, Minn., February 1974.

Federal Interagency Day Care Requirements. Washington, D.C.: United States Department of Health, Education, and Welfare, September 1968.

Felt, M. *Exploring Childhood: Program Overview and Catalog of Materials.* Newton, Mass.: Education Development Center, 1978.

Flood, J. E. "Parental Styles in Reading

Episodes with Young Children." *Reading Teacher* 30, no. 8 (May 1977): 864–867.

Florida Department of Education. *For Parents of Exceptional Children: A Bibliography.* Talahassee, Fla.: Florida Department of Education, 1975.

Forrester, B. J. "Parents as Educational Change Agents for Infants: Competencies not Credentials." Paper presented at the meeting of the Council on Exceptional Children, Washington, D.C., March 1972.

Forrester, B. J.; Brooks, G. P.; Hardge, B. M.; and Outlaw, D. D. *Materials for Infant Development.* Nashville, Tenn.: George Peabody College for Teachers, 1971.

Forrester, B. J.; Hardge, B. M.; Outlaw, D. D.; Brooks, G. P.; and Boismier, J. D. *Home Visiting with Mothers and Infants.* Nashville, Tenn.: Demonstration and Research Center for Early Education (DARCEE), George Peabody College, 1971.

Fraiberg, S. H. *Every Child's Birthright: In Defense of Mothering.* New York: Basic Books, 1977.

Fraiberg, S. H. *The Magic Years: Understanding and Handling the Problems of Early Childhood.* New York: Charles Scribner's Sons, 1959.

Fraser, J. G., ed. *The Puzzle of Parenting: How to Fit It Together. A Leadership Manual for Conducting Parent Programs in Early Childhood Development.* Columbia, S.C.: South Carolina Department of Parent Education, 1977.

Fraser, L. *A Cup of Kindness: A Book for Parents of Retarded Children.* Seattle, Wash.: Bernie Straub Publishing Co., Special Child Publications, 1973.

Freeberg, N. E., and Payne, D. T. "Parental Influence on Cognitive Development in Early Childhood." *Child Development* 38, no. 1 (1967): 65-87.

Freed, A. M. *T. A. for Tots.* Sacramento, Calif.: Jaemar Press, 1977.

French, M. A. *Odds and Ends: Learning Activities for Preschoolers.* Newark, Del.: University of Delaware Cooperative Extension Service, n.d.

Furstenberg, F. F. *Unplanned Parenthood: The Social Consequences of Teenage Childbearing.* Riverside, N.J.: Free Press, 1976.

Future Homemakers of America. "Teenage Parenting." *Teen Times,* January-February 1977.

Gallagher, J. J.; Haskins, R.; and Farran, D. C. "Poverty and Public Policy." In *The Family: Setting Priorities,* ed. T. B. Brazelton et al. New York: Science and Medicine Publishing Co., 1979.

Gallagher, J. J., et al. *Parent Involvement, Parent-Teacher Interaction and Child Development.* Urbana, Ill.: ERIC Clearinghouse

on Early Childhood Education, 1976. ED 125–773.

Garcia, A. "Developing Questioning Children: A Parent Program." *Teem Exchange* 2, no. 2 (1972): 3–7.

Gardner, R. *Boys and Girls Book about Divorce with an Introduction for Parents.* New York: Science House, 1970.

General Accounting Office. "Early Childhood Programs and Family Development Programs Improve the Quality of Life for Low-Income Families," Report of the Comptroller General of the United States. HRD 79–40. February 6, 1979.

Giesy, R. *A Guide for Home Visitors.* Nashville, Tenn.: Demonstration and Research Center for Early Education (DARCEE), George Peabody College, 1970.

Gilmer, B.; Miller, J. O.; and Gray, S. W. "Intervention with Mothers and Young Children: A Study of Intrafamily Effects." *DARCEE Papers and Reports* 4, no. 11 (1970). George Peabody College for Teachers, Nashville, Tenn.

Ginott, H. G. *Between Parent and Child: New Solutions to Old Problems.* New York: Macmillan, 1965.

Goldberg, R. J. "Caring for Children in the Family Context: New Patterns in Parent Behavior and Attitudes with Implications for the Helping Professions." Paper presented at the annual meeting of the American Association of Psychiatric Services for Children, Inc., 1978, Atlanta, Ga.

Golden, D. A., and Davis, J. G. "Counseling Parents after the Birth of an Infant with Down's Syndrome." *Children Today* 3 (1974): 7–11.

Golick, M. *A Parents' Guide to Learning Problems.* Côte St. Luc, Montreal, Quebec, Canada: Association for Children with Learning Disability, 1969.

Goodman, C. "PACE Family Treatment Centers: Narrative Descriptions." Bronx, N.Y.: Bronx Psychiatric Center, 1977.

Goodson, B. D., and Hess, R. D. *Parents as Teachers of Young Children.* Urbana, Ill.: ERIC Clearinghouse on Early Childhood Education, 1975. ED 136–967.

Gordon, I. J. *Baby to Parent, Parent to Baby.* New York: St. Martin's Press, 1977.

Gordon, I. J. "Developing Parent Power." In *Critical Issues in Research Related to Disadvantaged Children,* edited by E. Grotberg. Princeton, N.J.: Educational Testing Service, 1969a.

Gordon, I. J. "Parenting, Teaching, and Child Development." *Young Children* 31, no. 3 (March 1976): 173–183.

Gordon, I. J., ed. *Reaching the Child through Parent Education: The Florida Approach.* Gainesville, Fla.: University of Florida, College of Education, Institute for Development of Human Resources, 1969b.

Gordon, I. J. *Baby Learning through Baby Play.* New York: St. Martin's Press, 1970a.

Gordon, I. J. *Parent Involvement in Compensatory Education.* Urbana, Ill.: University of Illinois Press, 1970b.

Gordon, I. J. *Early Child Stimulation through Parent Education. Final Report.* Project No. PHS-R-306, Children's Bureau, Social and Rehabilitation Service, United States Department of Health, Education, and Welfare, 1971.

Gordon, I. J. *Dos and Don'ts of Parent Educating.* Gainesville, Fla.: Institute for Development of Human Resources, EDF 780, Seminar in Education, 1972a.

Gordon, I. J. "What Do We Know about Parents-As-Teachers?" Paper presented at the meetings of the American Educational Research Association, Chicago, Ill., April 1972b.

Gordon, I. J.; Greenwood, G. E.; Ware, W. B.; and Olmsted, P. P. *The Florida Parent Education Follow Through Program.* Gainesville, Fla.: Institute for Development of Human Resources, University of Florida and the Florida Educational Research and Development Council, 1974.

Gordon, I. J., and Guinagh, B. J. *A Home Learning Center Approach to Early Stimulation.* Gainesville, Fla.; University of Florida, College of Education, Institute for Development of Human Resources, 1969.

Gordon, I. J.; Guinagh, B. J.; and Jester, R. E. *Child Learning through Child Play: Learning Activities for Two and Three Year Olds.* New York: St. Martin's Press, 1972.

Gordon, I. J., and Jester, R. E. *Instructional Stretegies for Infant Stimulation.* Final Report on Project No. 5-RO1-MH-17347-02 to the National Institute of Mental Health. Washington, D.C.: United States Department of Health, Education, and Welfare, 1972.

Gordon, I. J., and Lally, J. R. *Intellectual Stimulation for Infants and Toddlers.* Gainesville, Fla.: University of Florida, College of Education, Institute for Development of Human Resources, 1967.

Gordon, I. J.; Olmsted, P. P.; Rubin, R. I.; and True, J. H. "How Has Follow Through Promoted Parent Involvement?" *Young Children* 34, no. 5 (July 1979): 49–53.

Gordon, S. *Living Fully: A Guide for Young People with a Handicap, Their Parents, Their Teachers, and Professionals.* New York: John Day & Co., 1975.

Gordon, S., and Wollin, M. *Parenting: A Guide for Young People.* New York: William H. Sadler, 1975.

Gordon, T. *Parent Effectiveness Training.* New York: Wyden Press, 1970.

Gordon, T. *P. E. T. in Action.* New York: Bantam Books, 1976.

Gotts, E. E. *The Home Visitor's Kit: Training and Practitioner Materials for Paraprofessionals in Family Settings.* New York: Human Sciences Press, 1977.

Gray, S. "Home Visiting Programs for Parents of Young Children." *DARCEE Papers and Reports* 5, no. 4 (1971). George Peabody College for Teachers, Nashville, Tenn.

Greenstein, B. L.; Garman, J. M.; and Sanford, J. S. "Sumner Mobile Pre-school: A Home-Centered Approach." *Young Children* 29 (1974): 155–160.

Grim, J. *Training Parents to Teach: Four Models.* Chapel Hill, N.C.: TADS, 1974.

Grissom, D. E. "Listening beyond Words: Learning from Parents in Conferences." *Childhood Education* 48, no. 30 (1971): 138–139.

Grollman, E. A. *Explaining Divorce to Children.* Boston: Beacon Press, 1969.

Grow, L. J. *Early Childrearing by Young Mothers: A Research Study.* Washington, D.C.: Child Welfare League of America, 1979.

Hafner, T. "The Cap and Gown Feeling." *The Exceptional Parent* 6, no. 1 (1976): 13–17.

Haimon, P. E. Child Care Pamphlets. Cleveland, Ohio: Press of Case Western Reserve University, 1972.

Haney, M. *Will Your Baby Learn to Read?* Springdale, Ark.: Springdale Education Association, 1978.

Hannibals. A. L. *Alphabet Animals.* Syracuse, N.Y.: Prodigy Press, 317 Allen St., Syracuse, N.Y., 1978.

Harrell, J., and Pizzo, P., eds. *Mothers in Paid Employment.* Washington, D.C.: Day Care and Child Development Council of America, 1973.

Harrison-Ross, P., and Wyden, B. *The Black Child: A Parent's Guide to Raising Happy and Healthy Children.* New York: Berkeley Publishing Co., 1974.

Head Start. "Head Start Newsletter." Washington, D.C.: Project Head Start, U.S. Department of Health, Education, and Welfare, Autumn 1977.

Head Start. "Impact of Parent Involvement Activities." Washington, D.C.: Project Head Start, U.S. Department of Health, Education, and Welfare, n.d.

Head Start. *Parent Involvement: Focus on Children with Special Needs.* Washington, D.C.: Project Head Start, U.S. Department of Health, Education, and Welfare, 1976.

Head Start. *Parent Involvement—A Workbook of Training Tips for Head Start Staff.* Washington, D.C.: Project Head Start, U.S. Department of Health, Education, and Welfare, 1968.

Heber, R.; Garber, H.; Harrington, S.; Hoffman, C.; and Fallender, C. *Rehabilitation of Families at Risk for Mental Retardation. A Progress Report.* Madison, Wis.: University of Wisconsin Rehabilitation Research and Training Center in Mental Retardation, 1972.

Heger, D. T. "A Supportive Service to Single Mothers and Their Children." *Children Today* 6 (1977): 2–4.

Heinicke, C. M. *Changes in the Preschool Child as a Function of Change in the Parent-Child Relationship.* Urbana, Ill.: ERIC Clearinghouse on Early Childhood Education, 1977. ED 138–377.

Hersh, S. P., and Levin, K. "How Love Begins Between Parent and Child." *Children Today* 7, no. 2 (Mar.-Apr. 1978): 2–6.

Hess, R. D. "Parental Behavior and Children's School Achievement: Implications for Head Start." In *Critical Issues in Research Related to Disadvantaged Children,* edited by E. Grotberg. Princeton, N.J.: Educational Testing Service, 1969.

Hess, R. D.; Beckum, L.; Knowles, R. T.; and Miller, R. "Parent-Training Program and Community Involvement in Day Care." In *Day Care: Resources for Decisions,* edited by E. Grotberg. Washington, D.C.: Office of Economic Opportunity, 1971.

Hess, R. D.; Shipman, V. C.; Brophy, J.; and Bear, R. B. *The Cognitive Environments of Urban Preschool Children.* Report to Children's Bureau, Social Security Administration, United States Department of Health, Education, and Welfare, 1968.

Hetherington, E. M.; Cox, M.; and Cox, R. "The Aftermath of Divorce." In *Mother/Child, Father/Child Relationships,* ed. J. H. Stevens, Jr., and M. Mathews. Washington, D.C.: National Association for the Education of Young Children, 1978a.

Hetherington, E. M.; Cox, M.; and Cox, R. "Family Interaction and the Social, Emotional and Cognitive Development of Children Following Divorce." Paper presented at Symposium on the Family, May 1978b, Washington, D.C.

Hetherington, E. M.; Cox, M.; and Cox, R. "Stress and Coping in Divorce: A Focus on Women." In *Psychology and Transition,* ed. J. Gullahorn. Washington, D.C.: V. H. Winston & Sons, 1978c.

Hetherington, E. M., and Deur, J. L. "The Effects of Father Absence on Child Development." *Young Children* 26, no. 4 (March 1971): 233.

High/Scope Educational Research Foundation. *Parental Support of Early Learning: Home Visitor Training.* Videotape Instructional Programs. Ypsilanti, Michigan, High/Scope Educational Research Foundation, 1973.

High/Scope Educational Research Foundation and Abt Associates, Inc. *The Home Start Summative Evaluation Report.* Washington, D.C.: United States Department of Health, Education, and Welfare, 1972.

Hindley, C. B. "Social Class Influence on the Development of Ability in the First Five Years." In *Proceedings of the XIV International Congress of Applied Psychology,* edited by G. Nielson, Child and Education 3 (1962): 29–41.

Hoffman, D. B. *Parent Participation in Preschool Day Care.* Atlanta, Ga.: Avatar Press, 1972.

Hoffman, M. L. "Father Absence and Conscience Development." *Developmental Psychology* 4 (1971): 400–406.

Hogan, J. C., and Schwartz, M. D. *Duties Owed to Children by a Parent, Teachers, the State, and All Others.* Lexington, Mass.: D. C. Heath & Co., 1979.

Honig, A. S. "Child Care Alternatives and Options for Parents." *Viewpoints in Teaching and Learning,* 1979a, in press.

Honig, A. S. *Fathering: A Bibliography.* Urbana, Ill.: ERIC Clearinghouse on Early Childhood Education, 1977. #164.

Honig, A. S. *Infant Development Projects: Problems in Intervention.* Washington, D.C.: Day Care and Child Development Council of America, 1972.

Honig, A. S. *Infant Education and Stimulation: A Bibliography.* Urbana, Ill.: ERIC Clearinghouse on Early Childhood Education, 1973.

Honig. A.S. "Parent Involvement and the Development of Children with Special Needs." In *Parenting Education of Handicapped Young Children,* ed. F. P. Connor, N. R. Glauberman, and S. R. Mann. New York: Department of Special Education, Teacher's College, Columbia University, 1979b.

Honig, A. S. "Parent Involvement in a Pediatric Out-Patient Waiting Room." Unpublished manuscript, Syracuse University, 1979c.

Honig, A. S. *A Review of Recent Infancy Research.* Washington, D.C.: Dingle Associates, 1978a.

Honig, A. S. "What We Need to Know to Help the Teenage Parent." *The Family Coordinator* 27 (1978b): 113–119.

Honig, A. S. "Working with Parents of Preschool Children," In *Parent Education and Intervention Handbook,* ed. R. Abidin. Springfield, Ill.: Charles C. Thomas, 1980.

Honig, A. S.; Caldwell, B. M.; and Tannenbaum, J. "Patterns of Information Processing Used by and with Young Children in a Nursery School Setting." *Child Development* 41 (1970): 1045–1065.

Honig, A. S., and Lally, J. R. *Infant Caregiving: A Design for Training.* Dr. A. S. Honig, College for Human Development, Syracuse University, 100 Walnut Pl., Syracuse, NY 13210, or Dr. J. R. Lally, 138 Edison Ave., Corte Madera, CA 94920. 1972.

Horejsi, C. R. "The St. Paul Family Centered Project Revisited—or Exploring an Old Gold Mine." Paper presented at the National Symposium on Home-Based Services for Children and Their Families, April 1979, University of Iowa.

Horton, D. "Structural Problems in the Head Start Parents' Program." Paper presented at the meeting of the American Educational Research Association symposium on "The Parent as Educational Agent," New York, February 1971.

Horton, D. M. "A Training Program for Mothers." Unpublished manuscript, DARCEE, George Peabody College for Teachers, Nashville, Tenn., n.d.

Hosey, C. "Yes, Our Son Is Still with Us." *Children Today* 2, no. 6 (Nov.-Dec. 1973): 14.

Howard, M. "Improving Services for Young Fathers." *Sharing*, Spring 1975a, pp. 45–53. Washington, D.C.: Child Welfare League of America.

Howard, M. *Only Human: Teenage Pregnancy and Parenthood.* New York: Seabury, 1975b.

Howard, N. K. *Mother-Child Home Learning Programs: An Abstract Bibliography.* ERIC publication catalogue No. 1300–21, Urbana, Ill.: College of Education Curriculum Laboratory, University of Illinois, March 1972.

Hubner, J. "Teaching Styles of Mothers of Low Income Spanish Surname Preschool Children." Unpublished master's thesis, San Francisco State College, 1970.

Hunt, J. McV.; Paraskevopoulos, J.; Schickedanz, O.; and Uzgiris, I. C. "Variations in the Mean Ages of Achieving Object Permanence under Diverse Conditions of Rearing." In *Infant Assessment and Intervention,* edited by B. Friedlander, G. Kirk, and G. Sterritt. New York: Brunner/Mazel, 1974, forthcoming.

Hutinger, P., and McKee, N. "The Baby Buggy: Bringing Services to Handicapped Rural Children." *Children Today* 8 (Jan.-Feb. 1979): 2–5.

Instructional Materials Center. *Preschool Learning Activities for the Visually Impaired Child.* Springfield, Ill.: Instructional Materials Center, n.d.

Jackson, R. K., and Stretch, H. A. "Perceptions of Parents, Teachers, and Administrators to Parental Involvement in Early Childhood Programs." *Alberta Journal of Educational Research* 22, no. 2 (June 1976): 129–139.

Jackson, R. H., and Terdal, L. "Parent Education Within a Pediatric Practice." *Journal of Pediatric Psychology* 3 (1978): 2–5.

Jenkins, C. G. "For Parents Particularly (II)." *Childhood Education* 55, no. 3 (Jan. 1979): 157–159.

Jenkins, J. K., and MacDonald, P. *Growing Up Equal.* Englewood Cliffs, N.J.: Prentice-Hall, 1979.

Jenkins, S. "Children of Divorce." *Children Today* 7, no. 2 (Mar.-Apr. 1978): 16–20.

Jester, R. E., and Bailey, J. "Hearing-Speech Scores on the Griffiths Mental Development Scale as a Function of Language Usage in the Home." In *Reaching the Child through Parent Education: The Florida Approach,* edited by I. J. Gordon. Gainesville, Fla.: Institute for the Development of Human Resources, University of Florida Research Reports, 1969, pp. 21–31.

Jew, W. "Helping Handicapped Infants and Their Families: The Delayed Development Project." *Children Today* 3 (1974): 7–10.

Johnson, D. L. "Houston Parent-Child Development Center." Paper presented at the biennial meeting of the Society for Research in Child Development, Philadelphia, Pa., March 1973.

Johnson, R. H. "Parent and Child Centers Early Intervention." *Head Start Newsletter* 6, no. 9 (December 1972-January 1973).

Johnson, V. M., and Werner, R. A. *A Step-By-Step Learning Guide for Retarded Infants and Children.* Syracuse, N.Y.: Syracuse University Press, 1975.

Johnson & Johnson Baby Products Co. *Infant Development Program: Birth—12 Months.* Great Neck, N.Y.: Johnson & Johnson Baby Products Co., 1976.

John Tracy Clinic. *Getting your Baby Ready to Talk: A Home Study Plan for Infant Language Development.* Los Angeles: John Tracy Clinic, 1968.

Jones, E. "Involving Parents in Children's Learning." *Childhood Education* 47, no. 3 (1970): 126–130.

Jones, M. H. "Intervention Programs for Children under Three Years Old." In *Infant Education,* ed. B. M. Caldwell and D. Stedman. Chapel Hill, N.C.: TADS, 1977.

Jones, P. S. "Parenthood Education in a City High School." *Children Today* 4 (1975): 7.

Kagan, J. *Infancy: Its Place in Human Development.* Cambridge, Mass.: Harvard University Press, 1978.

Kamii, C., and Lee-Katz, L. "Physics in Preschool Education: A Piagetian Approach." *Young Children* 34, no. 4 (May 1979): 4–9.

Kapfer, S. "Report of Selected Sessions from the Parents, Children and Continuity Conference." Washington, D.C.: Commission of the Administration for Children, Youth, and Families, U.S. Department of Health, Education, and Welfare, 1977.

Karnes, M. B. *Learning Language at Home.* Level I (3–5 yrs.), Level II (6–9 yrs.). Reston,

Va.: Council for Exceptional Children, 1978.

Karnes, M. B. *A New Role for Teachers: Involving the Entire Family in the Teaching of Preschool Disadvantaged Children*. Washington, D.C.: Bureau of Research, Office of Education, United States Department of Health, Education, and Welfare, 1969.

Karnes, M. B.; Hodgins, A. S.; Teska, J. A.; and Kirk, S. A. *Investigations of Classroom and At-Home Interventions. Final Report*. Washington, D.C.: Bureau of Research, Office of Education, United States Department of Health, Education, and Welfare, May 1969.

Karnes, M. B.; Studley, W. M.; Wright, W. R.; and Hodgins, A. S. "An Approach for Working with Mothers of Disadvantaged Preschool Children." *Merrill-Palmer Quarterly of Behavior and Development* 14, no. 2 (1968): 174–184.

Karnes, M. B.; Teska, J. A.; Hodgins, A. S.; and Badger, E. D. "Educational Intervention at Home by Mothers of Disadvantaged Infants." *Child Development* 41 (1970): 925–935.

Keniston, K., and Carnegie Council on Children. *All Our Children: The American Family under Pressure*. New York: Harcourt Brace Jovanovich, 1977.

"Kentucky Rural Child Care Project: Child Care and Parent Involvement in Litchfield." *Rural Child Newsletter* 1, no. 15 (1972).

Kifer, E. *The Relationship Between the Home and School in Influencing the Learning of Children*. Urbana, Ill.: ERIC Clearinghouse on Early Childhood Education, 1976. ED 133–073.

Klaus, M. H., and Kennell, J. H. *Maternal-Infant Bonding*. St. Louis, Mo.: C. V. Mosby Co., 1976.

Klaus, R. A., and Gray, S. W. "The Educational Training Program for Disadvantaged Children: A Report after Five Years." *Monographs of the Society for Research in Child Development* 33, no. 4 (1968).

Klein, C. *The Single Parent Experience*. New York: Avon, 1974.

Knox, L. *Parents Are People Too*. Nashville, Tenn.: Intersect Press, 1978.

Kroth, R. L. *Communicating with Parents of Exceptional Children: Improving Parent-Teacher Relationships*. Denver, Colo.: Love Publishing Co., 1975.

Kroth, R. L. "Parents—Powerful and Necessary Allies." *Teaching Exceptional Children* 10 (1978): 88–91.

Kruger, W. S. "Education for Parenthood and the Schools." *Children Today* 2 (1973): 4–7.

Kuipers, J.; Boger, R. B.; and Beery, M. "Parents as Primary Change Agents in Experimental Head Start Program of Language Intervention." Unpublished manuscript, Head Start Research Seminar, Washington, D.C., 1970.

LaCrosse, E. R. "Primary Influences on the Development of Competence: The Development of a Maternal Behavior Scale." In B. L. White (Chmn.), "The Preschool Project." Symposium presented at the biennial meeting of the Society for Research in Child Development, Santa Monica, Calif., March 1969.

Lally, J. R. "Classroom Progress Reports." Unpublished manuscript, Syracuse University Children's Center, 1969a.

Lally, J. R. "Selecting and Training Paraprofessionals for Work with Infants, Toddlers, and Their Families." In *Early Child Stimulation through Parent Education. Final Report*, edited by I. Gordon. Gainesville, Fla.: University of Florida, College of Education, Institute for Development of Human Resources, 1969b.

Lally, J..R. "Some Basic Information Anyone Who Works with Young Children Should Know." Unpublished manuscript, Syracuse University Children's Center, 1970.

Lally, J. R. "Child Care: Politics, Business, Research, and/or Service." *Journal of Clinical Child Psychology* 1, no. 1 (1972a): 10–11.

Lally, J. R. *The Family Development Research Program —a Program for Prenatal, Infant and Early Childhood Enrichment. Progress Report*. Office of Child Development, United States Department of Health, Education, and Welfare, 1972b.

Lally, J. R. *The Family Development Research Program—a Program for Prenatal Infant and Early Childhood Enrichment. Progress Report*. Office of Child Development, United States Department of Health, Education, and Welfare. 1973.

Lally, J. R. *The Family Development Research Program—a Program for Prenatal, Infant, and Early Childhood Enrichment. Progress Report*. Washington, D.C.: Office of Child Development, United States Department of Health, Education, and Welfare, 1974.

Lally, J. R., and Gordon, I. J. *Learning Games for Infants and Toddlers*. Syracuse, N.Y.: New Readers Press, 1977.

Lally, J. R., and Honig, A. S. "Education of Infants and Toddlers from Low-Income and Low-Education Backgrounds: Support for the Family's Role and Identity." In *Infant Assessments and Intervention*, edited by B. Friedlander, G. Kirk, and G. Sterritt. New York: Brunner/Mazel, 1975a.

Lally, J. R., and Honig, A. S. "The Family Development Research Program: A Program for Prenatal, Infant and Early Childhood Enrichment." In *The Preschool in Action: Exploring Early Childhood Programs*, ed. M. C. Day and R. D. Parker, 2nd ed. Boston:

Allyn and Bacon, 1977.

Lally, J. R.; Honig, A. S.; and Caldwell, B. M. "Training Paraprofessionals for Work with Infants and Toddlers." *Young Children* 28, no. 3 (1973): 173–182.

Lally, J. R., and Wright, C. J. "Parent Evaluation of Program (PEP) and Parent Evaluation of Program and Prognosis for Educational Responsibility (PEPPER)." Unpublished manuscripts, Syracuse University Children's Center, 1973.

Lamb, M. E. "Fathers: Forgotten Contributors to Child Development." *Human Development* 18 (1975): 245–266.

Lamb, M. E. *The Role of the Father in Child Development.* New York: John Wiley & Sons, 1976.

Lambie, D. Z. *Infant Education Curriculum Materials. Ypsilanti-Carnegie Infant Education Project. Preliminary Draft.* Ypsilanti, Mich.: High/Scope Educational Foundation, 1972.

Lambie, D. Z. "Mothers as Teachers." *High/ Scope Foundation Report,* 1973, pp. 6–10.

Lambie, D. Z.; Bond, J. T.; and Weikart, D. P. *Home Teaching with Mothers and Infants.* Ypsilanti, Mich.: High/Scope Educational Research Foundation, 1974.

Lane, M. B. *Education for Parenting.* Washington, D.C.: National Association for the Education of Young Children, 1975.

Lane, M. B.; Elzey, F. F.; and Lewis, M. S. *Nurseries in Cross-Cultural Education (NICE). Final Report.* San Francisco: San Francisco State College, School of Education, 1971.

Laosa, L. M. "Maternal Teaching Strategies in Chicano Families of Varied Educational and Socioeconomic Levels." *Child Development* 49 (1978): 1129–1135.

Larrabee, M. "Involving Parents in Their Children's Day Care Experience." *Children* 16, no. 4 (1969): 149–154.

Lasater, T. M.; Briggs, J.; Malone, P.; Gilliam, C. F.; and Weisburg, P. "The Birmingham Model for Parent Education." Paper presented at the biennial meeting of the Society for Research in Child Development, April 1975, Denver, Colo.

Lawrence, M. M. *Young Inner-City Families: Development of Ego Strength under Stress.* New York: Human Sciences Press, 1975.

Lazar, J. B., and Chapman, J. E. *A Review of the Present Status and Future Research Needs of Programs to Develop Parenting Skills.* Prepared for the Interagency Panel on Early Childhood Research and Development. Washington, D.C.: United States Department of Health, Education, and Welfare, 1972.

Lehane, S. *Help Your Baby Learn.* Englewood Cliffs, N.J.: Prentice-Hall, 1976.

Lesser, G. S.; Fifer, G.; and Clark, D. H. "Mental Abilities of Children in Different Social and Cultural Groups." *Monographs of the Society for Research in Child Development* 30, no. 4 (1965), Serial No. 102.

Levenson, P.; Hale, J.; Hollier, M.; and Tirado, C. "Serving Teenage Mothers and Their High-Risk Infants." *Children Today* 7 (July-Aug. 1978): 11–15.

Levenstein, P. "Cognitive Growth in Preschoolers through Verbal Interaction with Mothers." *American Journal of Orthopsychiatry* 40 (1970): 426–432.

Levenstein, P. "Learning through (and from) Mothers." *Childhood Education* 48, no. 3 (1971a): 130–134.

Levenstein, P. "The Mother-Child Home Program." In *The Preschool in Action: Exploring Early Childhood Programs,* ed. M. C. Day and R. D. Parker. 2nd ed. Boston: Allyn and Bacon, 1977.

Levenstein, P. *Verbal Interaction Project. Final Report.* Washington, D.C.: Children's Bureau, United States Department of Health, Education, and Welfare, 1971b.

Levenstein, P. *Model Programs Compensatory Education: Mother-Child Home Program.* Washington, D.C.: Office of Education, United States Department of Health, Education, and Welfare, 1972.

Levenstein, P. *Verbal Interaction Project/ Mother-Child Home Program. Manual for Replication of the Mother-Child Home Program.* 2nd ed. Freeport, N.Y.: Demonstration Project, 1973.

Levitt, E., and Cohen, S. "Parents as Teachers: A Rationale for Involving Parents in the Education of Their Young Handicapped Children." In *Current Topics in Early Childhood Education, Vol. I,* ed. L. G. Katz. Norwood, N.J.: Ablex, 1977.

Lief, N. R. *The First Year of Life: A Curriculum for Parenting Education.* New York: Keyway Books, 1979.

Ligon, E. M.; Barber, L. W.; and Williams, H. J. *Let Me Introduce Myself: A Guide for Parents of Infant Children.* Schenectady, N.Y.: Character Research Press, 1976.

Lillie, D. L.; Hayden, A. H.; Fredricks, H. D.; Baldwin, V. L.; Grove, D.; Shearer, M. S.; Weigerink, R.; and Parrish, V. *Training Parents to Teach: Four Models.* Greensboro, N.C.: Frank Porter Graham Child Development Center, University of North Carolina, n.d.

LINC. *100 Helping Hands from Parents.* Durham, N.C.: LINC Press, 1975.

Linnan, R. J., and Arassian, P. W. "Ethnic Comparisons of Environmental Process Predictors of Three Cognitive Abilities." Paper presented at the annual meeting of the American Educational Research Association, Chicago, Ill., April 1974.

Lynn, D. B. *The Father: His Role in Child De-*

velopment. Monterey, Calif.: Brooks/Cole Publishing Co., 1974.

MacLachlan, E. A., and Cole, E. P. "Learning about Children and Family Life: The Salvation Army Education for Parenthood Program." *Children Today* 7 (May-June 1978): 7–11.

Madden, J.; Levenstein, P.; and Levenstein, S. "Longitudinal Outcomes of Mother-Child Home Program." *Child Development* 47 (1976): 1015–1025.

Magnus, R. A. "Teaching Parents to Parent: Parent Involvement in a Residential Treatment Program." *Children Today* 3 (1974): 25–27.

Marans, A. E., and Lourie, R. "Hypotheses Regarding the Effects of Child Rearing Patterns on the Disadvantaged Child." In *The Disadvantaged Child,* edited by J. Hellmuth. Vol. 1. Seattle, Wash.: Special Child Publications, 1967.

Marx, O. H. *Physical Activities for Handicapped Children in the Home.* Iowa City, Iowa: University of Iowa, 1972.

Marzallo, J., and Lloyd, J. *Learning Through Play.* New York: Harper & Row, 1974.

Maybanks, S., and Bryce, M., eds. *Home-Based Services for Children and Families: Policy, Practice, and Research.* Springfield, Ill.: Charles C. Thomas, 1979.

Mayer, C. A.
1. "Understanding Young Children: Emotional Behavior and Development." #115.
2. "Understanding Young Children: Intellectual Development and Intellectual Disabilities." #118.
3. "Understanding Young Children: Language Development and Language Disabilities." #117.
4. "Understanding Young Children: Learning Development and Learning Disabilities." #116. (Prepared at the Alaska Treatment Center for Crippled Children and Adults, Anchorage, Alaska.) Urbana, Ill.: ERIC Clearinghouse on Early Childhood Education, 1974.

McAdoo, J. L. "Father-Child Interaction Patterns and Self-Esteem in Black Preschool Children." *Young Children* 34, no. 2 (January 1979): 46–53.

McCall, R. B., and Young, P. "Make Room for Daddy." *American Way,* March 1979.

McLaughlin, C. J. *The Black Parent's Handbook: A Guide to Healthy Pregnancy, Birth, and Child Care.* New York: Harcourt Brace Jovanovich, 1976.

Media Projects, Inc. *The Open Home.* New York: Media Projects, 1971.

Medinnus, G. R., ed. *Readings in the Psychology of Parent-Child Relations.* New York: Wiley, 1967.

MIDCO. *Perspectives on Parent Participation in Head Start: An Analysis and Critique.* Prepared under contract No. HEW-05-72-45. Washington, D.C.: Project Head Start, Office of Child Development, United States Department of Health, Education, and Welfare, November 1972.

Middleman, R. R. "A Service Pattern for Helping Unmarried Pregnant Teenagers." *Children* 17 (1970): 108–112.

Miller, M. S., and Baker, S. S. *Straight Talk to Parents: How You Can Help Your Child Get the Best Out of School.* New York: Stein and Day, 1976.

Miller, W. H. *Systematic Parent Training: Procedures, Cases, and Issues.* Campaign, Ill.: Research Press, n.d.

Mills, D. *Learning to Listen: A Book for Mothers of Hearing-Impaired Children.* Ontario, Canada: Ontario New Press, 1976.

Milner, E. A. "A Study of the Relationship between Reading Readiness and Grade One School Children and Patterns of Parent-Child Interaction" *Child Development* 22 (1951): 95–112.

Montemayor, R. *Parental Disciplinary Technique and the Development of Children's Moral Judgment.* Urbana, Ill.: ERIC Clearinghouse on Early Childhood Education, 1977. ED 153–717.

Morin, S. F., and Schultz, S. J. "The Gay Movement and the Rights of Children." *Journal of Social Issues* 34, no. 2 (1978).

Morreau, L. E. *Teaching Your Child.* St. Louis, Mo.: The Cemrel Institute, 1972.

Morris, A. G. "Conducting a Parent Education Program in a Pediatric Clinic Playroom." *Children Today* 3, no. 6 (Nov.-Dec. 1974): 11–17.

Morrison, G. S. *Parent Involvement in the Home, School, and Community.* Columbus, Ohio: Charles E. Merrill, 1978.

Munnion, C., and Grender, I., eds. *The Open Home: Early Learning Made Easy for Parents and Children.* New York: St. Martin's Press, 1976.

National Academy of Sciences. *Toward a National Policy for Children and Families.* Washington, D.C.: Advisory Committee on Child Development, National Research Council, 1976.

National Clearinghouse for Home-Based Services to Children. "Selected Bibliography on Home-Based Services for Children and Families" 1979; "Review of Research on Home-Based Services" 1979; "A Directory of Model Home-Based Social, Educational, and Health Services to Children and Families" 1979. Oakdale, Iowa: University of Iowa Institute of Child Behavior and Development.

National Federation of Settlements and Neighborhood Centers. *Preparing Teenag-*

ers for Parenthood: A Recommended "How to" Program Guide. New York: National Federation of Settlements and Neighborhood Centers, 1976.

National Right to Read Effort. "Reporting on Reading." Parents as Models for Reading 4, no. 4 (June 1978).

Nedler, S. E. "Working with Parents on the Run." Childhood Education 53, no. 3 (January 1977): 128–132.

Nedler, S. E., and McAfee, O. D. Working with Parents: Guidelines for Early Childhood and Elementary Teachers. Belmont, Calif.: Wadsworth Publishing Co., 1979.

Nelson, S. A. "Getting It Together." Sharing, Spring 1973, p. 1.

Nelson, S. A. "School-Age Parents." Children Today 2 (Mar.-Apr. 1973): 31–33.

Newman, S. Guidelines to Parent-Teacher Cooperation in Early Childhood Education. New York: Book-Lab, 1971.

Nimnicht, G. P. "Overview of a Responsive Program for Young Children." Unpublished manuscript, Far West Regional Laboratory for Education and Development, Berkeley, Calif. 1970.

Nimnicht, G. P. "A Model Program for Young Children That Responds to the Child." Unpublished manuscript, Far West Regional Laboratory for Education and Development, Berkeley, Calif., 1972.

Nimicht, G. P. "Workshop on Families, Child Education and Social Forces." Presented at Northern Illinois University, 1973.

Nimnicht, G. P.; Brown, E.; Addison, B.; and Johnson, S. Parent Guide: How to Play Learning Games with a Preschool Child. Morristown, N.J.: General Learning Corporation, 1971.

Office of Child Development. Parent and Child Centers: A Guide for the Development of Parent and Child Centers. Washington, D.C.: United States Department of Health, Education, and Welfare, 1968.

Office of Child Development. "Parents in Your Program." In Day Care No. 8: Serving Children with Special Needs, edited by S. Granato. Washington, D.C.: United States Department of Health, Education, and Welfare, 1972.

Office of Child Development. Children Today—Special Issue: Education for Parenthood 2, no. 2 (1973).

Offir, C. W. "Visual Speech: Their Fingers Do the Talking." Psychology Today 10 (1976): 73–78.

O'Keefe, R. A. Bibliography: Home-Based Child Development Program Resources. Washington, D.C.: Office of Child Development, United States Department of Health, Education, and Welfare, 1973a.

O'Keefe, R. A. The Child and Family Resource Program: An Overview. Washington, D.C.: U.S. Department of Health, Education, and Welfare, n.d. DHEW Publication No. (OHDS) 78-31087.

O'Keefe, R. A. The Home Start Demonstration Program: An Overview. Washington, D.C.: Office of Child Development, United States Department of Health, Education, and Welfare, February 1973b.

O'Keefe, R. A. "What Head Start Means to Families." Washington, D.C.: Home Start and the Child and Family Resource Program, Head Start Bureau, Commission on the Administration of Children, Youth, and Families, U.S. Department of Health, Education, and Welfare, 1978.

Olmsted, P. P., and Jester, R. E. "Mother-Child Interaction in a Teaching Situation." Unpublished manuscript, Institute for the Development of Human Resources, College of Education, University of Florida, Gainesville, Fla., 1972.

Oppel, W. C., and Royston, A. B. "Teenage Births: Some Social, Psychological, and Physical Sequelae." American Journal of Public Health 61 (1971): 751–756.

Packer, A. B.; Resnick, M. B.; Resnick, J. L.; and Wilson, J. M. "An Elementary School with Parents and Infants." Young Children 34, no. 2 (January 1979): 4–9.

Painter, G. Teach Your Baby. New York: Simon & Schuster, 1971.

Pannor, R.; Massarik, F.; and Evans, B. The Unmarried Father: New Approaches for Unmarried Young Parents. New York: Springer, 1971.

Parent-Child Development Center. Progress Report 1975. Houston, Tex.: Parent-Child Development Center, University of Houston, April 1975.

Parent Cooperative Preschools International. Brochure. 20551 Lakeshore Rd., Baie d'Urfe 850, Quebec, Canada.

"Parent Education TV Series." Children Today 7 (Nov.-Dec. 1978): 28–29.

Parents as Resource Project. Recipes for Fun. Recipes for Holiday Fun. Workshop Procedures. Winnetka, Ill.: PAR Project, 1971.

Parents Without Partners. The Single Parent. Journal published for single parents. Parents Without Partners, 7910 Woodmont Avenue., Washington, DC 20014.

Parker, R., and Kass, R. E., eds. 80 booklets in Spanish on childrearing techniques. New York: Random House, Institute for the Development of Human Resources, 1975.

Parker, S., and Kleiner, R. J. "Characteristics of Negro Mothers in Single Headed Households." Journal of Marriage and Family 28 (1966): 507–513.

Patterson, G. R. Families: Applications of Social Learning to Family Life. Champaign, Ill.:

Research Press, 1971.

Patterson, G. R. *Living with Children: New Methods for Parents and Teachers.* rev. ed. Champaign, Ill.: Research Press, 1976.

Pavenstedt, E. "A Comparison of the Child-rearing Environment of Upper-Lower and Lower-Lower Class Families." *American Journal of Orthopsychiatry* 35 (1965): 89–98.

Pavloff, G., and Wilson, G. *Adult Involvement in Child Development for Staff and Parents: A Training Manual.* Atlanta, Ga.: Humanics Associates, 1972.

Peck, E., and Granzig, W. *The Parent Test: How to Measure and Develop Your Talent for Parenthood.* New York: G. P. Putnam's Sons, 1978.

Perske, R. *New Directions for Parents of Persons Who Are Retarded.* Nashville, Tenn.: Abingdon Press, 1973.

Pickarts, E., and Fargo, J. *Parent Education.* New York: Appleton-Century-Crofts, 1971.

Piers, M. *How to Work with Parents.* Bulletin No. 5-1121. Science Research Associates, 259 East Erie Street, Chicago, Ill., 60611, 1955.

Pierson, D. E. *The Brookline Program for Infants and Their Families—Program Report.* Brookline, Mass.: Brookline Early Education Project, 1973.

PMIC. *Parenting in 1977.* Southwest Educatioal Development Laboratory, 211 E. 7th St., Austin, TX 78701. 1977.

Powell, D. R. "The Interpersonal Relationship Between Parents and Caregivers." *American Journal of Orthopsychiatry* 48 (1978): 680–689.

Prescott, E. *A Pilot Study of Day Care Centers and Their Clientele.* Washington, D.C.: United States Government Printing Office, Children's Bureau publication No. 428, United States Department of Health, Education, and Welfare, 1965.

Project Head Start. *Parents Are Needed,* no. 6. Community Action Program, Washington, D.C.: Office of Economic Opportunity, 17 pp., n.d.

Puit, D., and Totman, N. "Having of Wonderful Ideas." In *Project Change Mini-Book-a-Month,* edited by L. Hammond. 2, no. 2 (1974).

Pushaw, D., ed. *Teach Your Child to Talk: A Parent Handbook.* Cincinnati: CDBCO Standard Publishing Company, 1969.

Rabinowitz, M.; Weiner, G.; and Jackson, C. R. *In the Beginning: A Parent Guide of Activities and Experiences for Infants from Birth to Six Months.* Book 1. New Orleans: Parent Child Development Center, 1973.

Radin, N. "Three Degrees of Parent Involvement in a Preschool Program: Impact on Mothers and Children." *Child Development* 43 (1972): 1355–1364.

Radin, N., and Glasser, P. "The Use of Parental Questionnaires with Culturally Disadvantaged Families." *Journal of Marriage and the Family* 27 (1965): 373–382.

Radin, N., and Kamii, C. K. "The Child-Rearing Attitudes of Disadvantaged Negro Mothers and Some Educational Implications." *The Journal of Negro Education* 34 (1965): 138–146.

Raifner, S., and Drouillard, R. *Get a Wiggle On: A Guide for Helping Visually Impaired Children Grow.* Mason, Mich.: Ingham Intermediate School District, 1975.

Randall, R. *Early Childhood Education System for 3 and 4 Year Old Migrant Children. Evaluation Report.* McAllen, Tex.: Southwest Educational Development Laboratory, 1969. ERIC Document No. ED 043370.

Recruitment Leadership and Training Institute. *The Role of Parents as Teachers.* Philadelphia: Temple University, 1975.

Reid, H. "The Warm Line: A Telephone Counseling Service for Parents." *Pediatric Annals* 6 (1977): 663–669.

Resnick, M. "The Relationship between Language Ability and Intellectual and Behavioral Functioning on Environmentally Disadvantaged Two and Three Year Olds." Unpublished doctoral dissertation, University of Florida, 1973.

Rheingold, H. L. "The Measurement of Maternal Care." *Child Development* 31 (1960): 565–575.

Rice, M. F., and Flatter, C. H. *Help Me Learn: A Handbook for Teaching Children from Birth to Third Grade.* Englewood Cliffs, N.J.: Prentice-Hall, 1979.

Rich, D., and Jones, C. *A Family Affair: Education, Families and the Helping Professions in Partnership.* Washington, D.C.: Home and School Institute, Trinity College, 1977.

Richard, J. "The Parent Place." *Human Behavior* 7 (1978): 36–37.

Riddle, D. I. *Gay Parents and Child Custody Issue.* Urbana, Ill.: ERIC Clearinghouse on Early Childhood Education, 1977. ED 147–746.

Rinn, R. C., and Markle, A. *Positive Parenting.* Cambridge, Mass.: Research Media, 1977.

Robison, H. "Working with Parents: Mutual Respect." In *Exploring Teaching in Early Childhood Education,* ed. H. Robison. Boston: Allyn and Bacon, 1977.

Roe, A., and Siegelman, M. "A Parent-Child Relations Questionnaire." *Child Development* 34 (1963): 355–369.

Rowen, B. *Tuning into Your Child: Awareness Training for Parents.* Atlanta, Ga.: Humanics Press, 1975.

Ryan, T. J. *Promoting Child Development through a Program of Home Visiting. Progress Report.* Ottawa, Canada: Carleton Uni-

96

versity, 1972.

Sale, J. S., and Torres, Y. L. *I'm Not Just a Baby-Sitter.* Descriptive report of the Community Family Day Care Project. Pasadena, Calif.: Pacific Oaks College, 1971.

Salk, L. *Preparing for Parenthood: Understanding Your Feelings about Pregnancy, Childbirth and Your Baby.* New York: Bantam Books, 1974.

Salk, L. *What Every Child Would Like His Parents to Know to Help Him with the Emotional Problems of His Everyday Life.* New York: McKay, 1972.

Santrock, J. W. "Father Absence, Perceived Maternal Behavior, and Moral Development in Boys." *Child Development* 46 (1975): 753–757.

Santrock, J. W. "Paternal Absence, Sex Typing, and Identification." *Developmental Psychology* 2 (1970): 264–272.

Schaefer, E. S. "Child Development Research and the Educational Revolution: The Child, the Family, and the Education Profession." Paper presented at the annual meeting of the American Educational Research Association, New Orleans, La., February 1973.

Schaefer, E. S. *Manual for Test Administration: The Schaefer Classroom Behavior Inventory.* Princeton, N.J.: Educational Testing Service, n.d.

Schaefer, E. S. "Parents as Educators: Evidence from Cross Sectional, Longitudinal and Intervention Research." *Young Children,* 27 (1972): 227–239.

Schaefer, E. S. *Professional Paradigms in Programs for Parents and Children.* Urbana, Ill.: ERIC Clearinghouse on Early Childhood Education, 1977. ED 147–033.

Schaefer, E. S., and Aaronson, M. R. *Home Behavior Inventory.* Washington, D.C.: National Institute of Mental Health, United States Department of Health, Education, and Welfare, n.d.

Schaefer, E. S., and Bell, R. Q. "Development of a Parental Attitude Research Instrument." *Child Development* 29 (1958): 339–361.

Scheinfeld, D. R. "On Developing Developmental Families." In *Critical Issues in Research Related to Disadvantaged Children,* edited by E. Grotberg. Princeton, N.J.: Educational Testing Service, 1969.

Scheinfeld, D. R.; Bowles, D.; Tuck, S.; and Gold, R. "Parents' Values, Family Networks, and Family Development: Working with Disadvantaged Families." Paper presented at the annual meeting of the American Orthopsychiatric Association, New York, April 1969. *Research Report* 6, no. 9. Institute for Juvenile Research, Chicago, Ill.

Schlesinger, B. "Single-Parent Fathers: A Research Review." *Children Today* 7 (1978): 12–13.

Sears, R. R.; Maccoby, E. E.; and Levin, H. *Patterns of Child Rearing.* Evanston, Ill.: Row, Peterson, 1957.

Segal, M. *From Birth to One Year.* Nova University series. B. L. Winch & Associates, 45 Hitching Post Dr., Bldg. 2, Rolling Hills Estates, CA 90274. 1974.

Segal, M., and Adcock, D. *From One to Two Years.* Nova University series. B. L. Winch & Associates, 45 Hitching Post Dr., Bldg. 2, Rolling Hills Estates, CA 90274. 1976.

Segal, M., and Adcock, D. *Play and Learning.* Nova University series. B. L. Winch & Associates, 45 Hitching Post Dr., Bldg. 2, Rolling Hills Estates, CA 90274. 1979.

Segal, M., and Adcock, D. *Social Competence.* Nova University series. B. L. Winch & Associates, 45 Hitching Post Dr., Bldg. 2, Rolling Hills Estates, CA 90274. 1979.

Segner, L., and Patterson, C. *Ways to Help Babies Grow and Learn.* Denver, Colo.: World Press, 1970.

Shearer, M. S., and Shearer, D. E. "The Portage Project: A Model for Early Childhood Education." *Exceptional Children* 39 (1972): 210–217.

Shere, E., and Kastenbaum, R. "Mother-Child Interaction in Cerebral Palsy: Environmental and Psychological Obstacles to Cognitive Development." *Genetic Psychology Monographs* 73 (1966): 225–335.

Shoemaker, L. P. *Parent and Family Life Education for Low Income Families: A Guide for Leaders.* Washington, D.C.: United States Department of Health, Education, and Welfare, 1965.

Shure, M. B., and Spivack, G. *Problem-Solving Techniques in Childrearing.* San Francisco: Jossey-Bass, 1978.

Sitnick, V.; Rushmer, N.; and Arpan, R. *Parent-Infant Communication: A Program of Clinical and Home Training for Parents and Hearing-Impaired Infants.* Portland, Oreg.: Good Samaritan Hospital and Medical Center, n.d.

Slaughter, D. T. "A Dimension of the Family as Educator: Mother as Teacher." Paper presented at the biennial meeting of the Society for Research in Child Development, March 1979, San Francisco.

Slaughter, D. T. "Maternal Antecedents of the Academic Achievement Behavior of Negro Head Start Children." Paper presented at the annual meeting of the American Psychological Association, San Francisco, Calif., September 1968.

Smith, H. W. *Survival Handbook for Preschool Mothers.* Chicago: Follett Publishing Co., 1978.

Smith, R. A. *How Your Child Learns to Talk.* Columbia, S.C.: South Carolina Department of Education, 1977.

Spock, B. M. *Dr. Spock Talks with Mothers: Growth and Guidance.* Boston: Houghton-Mifflin, 1955.

Spock, B. M. *Raising Children in a Difficult Time: A Philosophy of Parental Leadership and High Ideals.* New York: W. W. Norton, 1974.

Sprigle, H. A. "Who Wants to Live on Sesame Street?" *Young Children* 28, no. 2 (1972): 91–96.

SRCD. *Bibliography: Child Development and Social Policy.* Ann Arbor, Mich.: Bibliography Committee on Child Development and Social Policy, 1979.

Sroufe, A. *Knowing and Enjoying Your Baby.* Englewood Cliffs, N.J.: Prentice-Hall, 1978.

Sroufe, A., and Waters, E. "Attachment as an Organizational Construct." *Child Development* 48 (1977): 1184–1199.

Stein, L. "Techniques for Parent Discussion in Disadvantaged Areas." *Young Children* 22, no. 4 (1967): 210–217.

Stein, S. *The Open Home: Early Learning Made Easy for Parents and Children.* New York: St. Martin's Press, 1976.

Stein, S., and Lottick, S. T. *Three, Four, Open the Door: Creative Fun for Young Children.* Chicago: Follett Publishing Co., 1971.

Stern, C.; Marshall, J.; and Edwards, J. "Increasing the Effectiveness of Parents-as-Teachers." Paper presented at the meetings of the American Educational Research Association, New York, 1971.

Stevens, J. H., Jr. "Current Directions in the Study of Parental Facilitation of Children's Cognitive Development." *Educational Horizons* 50, no. 2 (1973): 62–66.

Stevens, J. H., Jr. *Training Parents as Home Teachers: A Review of Research.* Urbana, Ill.: ERIC Clearinghouse on Early Childhood Education, 1977. ED 147–014.

Stevens, J. H., Jr., and Mathews, M., eds. *Mother/Child, Father/Child Relationships.* Washington, D.C.: National Association for the Education of Young Children, 1978.

Stewart, J. C. *Counseling Parents of Exceptional Children.* Columbus, Ohio: Charles E. Merrill, 1978.

Streissguth, A., and Bee, H. "Mother-Child Interactions and Cognitive Development in Children." *Young Children* 27 (1972): 154–183.

Strodtbeck, F. L. "The Hidden Curriculum in the Middle-Class Home." In *Learning and the Educational Process,* edited by J. D. Krumboltz. Skokie, Ill.: Rand McNally & Co., 1965.

Stuart, I., and Abt, L. E., eds. *Children of Separation and Divorce.* New York: Viking Press, 1972.

Sumpter, D., and Metger, R. *How and What Your Child Learns Through Play.* Columbia, S.C.: South Carolina Department of Education, 1977.

Swan, R. W., and Stavros, H. "Child-Rearing Practices Associated with the Development of Cognitive Skills of Children in Low Socio-Economic Areas." *Early Child Development and Care* 2 (1973): 23–38.

Swirsky, "The Parent as Professional." *The Exceptional Parent* 7 (1977): 44–49.

Talbot, N. B. *Raising Children in Modern America: What Parents and Society Should Be Doing for Their Children.* Boston: Little Brown & Co., 1976.

"Teenage Parenting." *Teen Times* 32, no. 3 (January 1977).

Thompson, J. M., and Patrick, R. *The Implications of Parent Effectiveness Training for Foster Parents.* Urbana, Ill.: ERIC Clearinghouse on Early Childhood Education, 1970. ERIC Document No. ED 052821.

Thompson, M. "Helping Parents Understand Program Activities in a Day Care Center." In *Day Care: An Expanding Resource for Children.* New York: Child Welfare League of America, 1965.

Thune, J. M. "Grandparents for Children. Senior Citizen's Inc., Nashville, Tennessee." In *Programs for Infants and Young Children: Part I. Education and Day Care.* Washington, D.C.: Appalachian Regional Commission, 1970.

Top of Alabama Regional Council of Governments (TARCOG) Homestart Program Brochure. Huntsville, Ala.: Top of Alabama Regional Council of Governments, 1972.

Tuck, S. "A Model for Working with Black Fathers." Paper presented at the annual meeting of the American Orthopsychiatric Association in San Francisco, Calif., 1969. *Research Report* 6, no. 9. Institute for Juvenile Research, Chicago, Ill.

Tuckman, J., and Regan, R. A. "Intactness of the Home and Behavioral Problems in Children" *Journal of Child Psychology and Psychiatry* 7 (1966): 225–233.

Turnbull, A. P., and Turnbull, H. R. *Parents Speak Out: Views from the Other Side of the Two-Way Mirror.* Columbus, Ohio: Charles E. Merrill, 1978.

University of the State of New York. *Learning Experiences at Home: Reinforcement for the Early School Program.* Albany, N.Y.: State University of New York, n.d.

Vaughan, V. C., and Brazelton, T. B., eds. *The Family—Can It Be Saved?* Chicago: Yearbook Medical Publishers, 1976.

Wachs, T. D.; Uzgiris, I. C.; and Hunt, J. McV. "Cognitive Development in Infants of Different Age Levels and from Different Environmental Backgrounds: An Explanatory Investigation." *Merrill-Palmer Quarterly* 17 (1971): 283–317.

Waggonseller, B. R.; Burnett, M.; Salzberg, B.; and Burnett, J. *The Art of Parenting: A Complete Training Kit.* Champaign, Ill.: Research Press, 1977.

Wallat, C., and Goldman, R. M. *Home/School/Community Interaction: What We Know and Why We Don't Know More.* Columbus, Ohio: Charles E. Merrill, n.d.

Warner, D., and Quill, J. *Beautiful Junk.* Washington, D.C.: Project Head Start, Office of Child Development, United States Department of Health, Education, and Welfare, 1969.

Washington, K. R. "SUCCESS: A Parent Effectiveness Approach for Developing Urban Children's Self-Concepts." *Young Children* 32, no. 5 (July 1977): 5–10.

Watts, J. C.; Barnett, I. C.; and Halfar, C. *Environment, Experience and Development in Early Childhood.* Final Report. Grant No. CG-9916 to the Office of Economic Opportunity, Head Start Division, 1973.

Weaver, C. "Parent-Teacher Communication." *Childhood Education* 3 (1968): 420.

Weigerink, R. "Parent Involvement in Preschool Programs for the Handicapped: A National View." Paper presented at the Parent Education and Involvement Conference, June 1979, University of North Carolina, Chapel Hill.

Weikart, D. P. *Ypsilanti-Carnegie Education Project: Progress Report.* Ypsilanti, Mich.: Department of Research and Development, Ypsilanti Public Schools, 1969.

Weikart, D. P. "Early Childhood Special Education for Intellectually Subnormal and/or Culturally Different Children." Paper prepared for the National Leadership Institute in Early Childhood Development, Washington, D.C., October 1971a.

Weikart, D. P. "Learning through Parents: Lessons for Teachers." *Childhood Education* 11 (1971b): 119–236.

Weikart, D. P.; Deloria, D. J.; Lawser, S. A.; and Weigerink, R. *Longitudinal Results of the Ypsilanti Perry Preschool Project.* Ypsilanti, Mich.: High/Scope Educational Research Foundation, 1970, pp. D-1—D-14.

Weikart, D.; Rogers, L.; Adcock, C.; and McClelland, D. "Home Visits." In *The Cognitively Oriented Curriculum.* Washington, D.C.: The National Association for the Education of Young Children, 1971.

Wheelock College Center for Parenting Studies, Nine papers from a Symposium on Children and Divorce. Boston: Wheelock College, 1978.

Whelan, E., and Higgins, G. *Teenage Childrearing: Extent and Consequences.* Washington, D.C.: Child Welfare League of America/Consortium on Early Childbearing and Childrearing, 1973.

White, B. L. "Center for Parent Education Newsletter," vol. 1, no. 2 (February 1979).

White, B. L. *The First Three Years of Life.* Englewood Cliffs, N.J.: Prentice-Hall, 1975.

White, B. L. "Guidelines for Parent Education." Paper presented at the Planning Education Conference, September 1977, Flint, Mich.

Wight, B., and Corey, V. "Infant Learning Project." Washington, D.C.: Maternal and Child Health Service, U.S. Department of Health, Education, and Welfare, 1974.

Willerman, L.; Broman, S. H.; and Fiedler, M. "Infant Development, Preschool IQ, and Social Class." *Child Development* 41, no. 1 (March 1970).

Williams, T. M. *Infant Care: Abstracts of the Literature,* 1972. *Infant Care: Abstracts of the Literature-Supplement,* 1974. Washington, D.C.: Consortium on Early Childbearing and Childrearing, Research Utilization and Information Sharing Project.

Willmon, B. "Parent Participation as a Factor in the Effectiveness of Head Start Programs." *The Journal of Educational Research* 62, no. 9 (1969): 406–410.

Wilms, B. *Crunchy Bananas and Other Great Recipes.* Latton, Utah: Sagamore Books, 1975.

Wilson, A. L. *A Predictive Analysis of Early Parental Attachment Behavior.* Urbana, Ill.: ERIC Clearinghouse on Early Childhood Education, 1977. ED 140–955.

Wilson, G. B., and Wingate, B. *Parents and Teachers: Humanistic Educational Techniques to Facilitate Communication Between Parents and Staff of Educational Programs.* Atlanta, Ga.: Humanics Press, 1974.

Wilson, G. B., and Pavloff, G. *Adult Involvement in Child Development for Staff and Parents.* Atlanta, Ga.: Humanics, 1972.

Wilt, J., and Watson, T. *Touch!* Waco, Tex.: Creative Resources, 1977.

Wittes, G., and Radin, N. *Helping Your Child to Learn: The Learning through Play Approach.* San Rafael, Calif.: Dimensions Publishing Co., 1969.

Wolf, R. M. "The Identification and Measurement of Environmental Process Variables Related to Intelligence." Unpublished doctoral dissertation, University of Chicago, April 1964.

Woodard, S. L. "Ten Ways to Help Your Child Succeed." *Ebony Magazine,* October 1977, pp. 52–56.

Worley, S. E. "Parents Are Also Teachers." *Childhood Education* 43, no. 6 (1967): 341–344.

Wortis, J., et al. "Child Rearing Practices in a Low Socio-economic Group." *Pediatrics* 24 (1963): 298–307.

Wright, C. J. "Implementation of the Home

Visit Program." Paper presented at a Home Visitor Workshop, State of North Carolina, Department of Administration, Office of Child Development, Montreat, N.C., July 1973.

Yarrow, L. J.; Rubenstein, J. L.; and Pedersen, F. A. "Dimensions of Early Stimulation: Differential Effects on Infant Development." Symposium presented at the biennial meeting of the Society for Research in Child De-velopment, Minneapolis, Minn., April 1971.

Zigler, E. "The Environmental Mystique: Training the Intellect Versus Development of the Child." *Childhood Education* 46, no. 8 (1970): 402–412.

Zitner, R., and Hayden, S. H. *Teenage Parents and Their Support Services.* Washington, D.C.: Child Welfare League of America, 1979.

Films

Concept Media. "First Two and a Half Years"—1973, #S109; "Two and a Half to Six years"—1975, #S115. Human Development Series. Concept Media, P.O. Box 19542, Irvine, CA 92714.

Concept Media. "The Handicapped Child: Infancy Through Preschool"—1977, #S125. Concept Media, P.O. Box 19542, Irvine, CA 92714.

Davidson Films. "Nurturing" and "In the Beginning: The Process of Development," with Bettye M. Caldwell. Davidson Films, 3701 Buchanan St., San Francisco, CA 94123.

Education Development Center. "Somewhere to Go," (concerns of parents of Down's Syndrome children). Education Development Center, 39 Chapel St., Newton, MA 02160.

Ferraro, G. "Parents and Children: A Positive Approach to Child Management," 16 mm., color, 24 minutes, #1958 purchase, #1959 rental. Research Press Films, Box 3177E, Champaign, IL 61820.

Filmmakers Library. "Out of the Mouths of Babes: The Acquisition of Lanugage." Filmmakers Library, 290 W. End Ave., New York, NY 10023.

Guidance Associates. *Parenthood: A Series,* 8 filmstrips: "Preparing for Parenthood," "Pregnancy," "Preparing to Give Birth," "Birth," "Adjusting to the New Baby," "Child Development: The Preschool Years," and "Skills for Parents," with Discussion Guide by Alice S. Honig. Guidance Associates, 757 Third Ave., New York, NY 10017. 1978.

High/Scope Educational Research Foundation. Parental Support of Early Learning Films: "Opportunities for Learning," "Babies Like Attention," "A Special Kind of Mother," "Learning Through Problems: A Baby's Point of View," "Cans: Toys for Learning," and "Responding to Baby's Actions." High/Scope Educational Reserach Foundation, 600 N. River, Ypsilanti, MI 48197. 1978.

Modern Talking Picture Service, Inc. "Jenny Is a Good Thing" and "Parents Are Teachers Too." Modern Talking Picture Service, Inc., 1901 L St., N.W., Washington, DC 20036 (16 locations across the country).

Parents' Magazine. *Everyday Problems of Young Children. Prenatal Care: Preparing for Parenthood. The First 18 Months: From Infant to Toddler.* (A series of three sound and color filmstrip sets for parents and caregivers.) 1973a.

Parents' Magazine. *Understanding Early Childhood Ages 1 through 6.* (A series of four sound and color filmstrip sets on child development and behavior.) 1973b.

Parents' Magazine Films. "Even Love Is Not Enough: Children with Handicaps," filmstrip series. Parents' Magazine Films, 52 Vanderbilt Ave., New York, NY 10017. 1975.

Parents' Magazine Films. "Mothers and Fathers," "Parent Involvement: A Program for Teachers and Educators," and "The School Age Parent." Sound and color filmstrips. Parents' Magazine Films, 52 Vanderbilt Ave., New York, NY 10017.

Polymorph Films. "Adapting to Parenthood," "Call Me Mama" (mothering a toddler), "Mothers after Divorce," and "Stepparenting: New Families, Old Ties." Polymorph Films, 331 Newbury St., Boston, MA 02115. 1978.

WNET. "Footsteps" (videotape), series on TV Channel 13 in New York. WNET, 856 W. 58th St., New York, NY 10019.

Index of Names

Selected NAEYC Publications

If you found this book helpful, you may want to order these and other NAEYC publications.

Code #	Title	Price
214	Activities for School-Age Child Care	$3.85
132	The Block Book	$3.85
200	Careers with Young Children: Making Your Decision	$4.40
213	Caring: Supporting Children's Growth	$2.20
402S	Cómo Reconocer un Buen Programa de Educación Pre-Escolar	$ .30
313	Cultural Awareness: A Resource Bibliography	$5.20
121	Developmental Screening in Early Childhood: A Guide	$2.75
108	Education for Parenting	$3.30
215	A Festival of Films	$2.00
124	"The Good Life" for Infants and Toddlers	$2.00
302	A Guide to Discipline	$1.65
210	The Idea Box	$6.25
211	The Infants We Care For	$2.20
101	Let's Play Outdoors	$1.10
312	Mother/Child, Father/Child Relationships	$5.20
308	Mud, Sand, and Water	$2.20
102	Piaget, Children, and Number	$2.20
129	Play: The Child Strives Toward Self-Realization	$2.75
309	Science with Young Children	$3.55
128	The Significance of the Young Child's Motor Development	$2.45
402E	Some Ways of Distinguishing a Good Early Childhood Program	$ .30

Order from: NAEYC
1834 Connecticut Avenue, N.W.
Washington, DC 20009

All prices include postage and handling. Please enclose full payment for orders under $10.

For information about these and other NAEYC publications, write for a free publications brochure.